T0099214

Women Times Three

Women Times Three:

Writers, Detectives, Readers

Kathleen Gregory Klein, editor

Bowling Green State University Popular Press
Bowling Green, Ohio 43403

Copyright © 1995 Bowling Green State University Popular Press

Library of Congress Cataloging-in-Publication Data
Women times three : writers, detectives, readers / Kathleen Gregory
    Klein, editor.
        p.   cm.
    Includes bibliographical references (p.   ).
    ISBN 0-87972-681-4. -- ISBN 0-87972-682-2 (pbk.)
    1. Detective and mystery stories, American--Women authors--History
and criticism. 2. Detective and mystery stories, English--Women
authors--History and criticism. 3. Women detectives in literature.
4. Women and literature--United States--History--20th century.
5. Women and literature--Great Britain--History--20th century.
6. Women--Books and reading. 7. Feminism and literature. 8. Women
in literature. 9. Authors and readers.   I. Klein, Kathleen
Gregory, 1946-   .
PS374.D4W66   1995
813'.0872089287--dc20   95-17734
                                                                CIP

Cover design by Laura Darnell Dumm

This book is dedicated to my sisters
Joanne Mary Gregory
and
Regina Mary Buehl
and, as always, to
Rick Klein

Contents

Preface

These essays explore the range of relationships among women writers, the women detectives and women-centered novels they create, and women readers. Following an overview essay by the editor, they are arranged according to the definition of woman reader which the essay presents. The first essays define the woman reader as the author of the essay, tracing how one specifically identified reader of a woman writer creating a woman detective works, herself, to create a text and a context. The second group of essays explores the ways in which a specified group of readers—lesbians, feminist literary critics, for example—has or might read texts in which their politics give them a particular interest. The third set of essays poses the techniques, responses, needs, and preferences of the hypothetical woman reader engaged—either positively or critically—with a woman-authored, woman-focused text/detective. The careful reader of this volume will discover that all of the essays are, at least in some sense, personally based as well as concerned with the hypothetical woman reader. And, certainly, all employ feminist literary theory and criticism in considering the connections among women writers, women detectives/texts, and women readers.

Women Times Women Times Women

Kathleen Gregory Klein

Triangle.

A closed plane figure.

Love triangles. Usually three people in shifting patterns of two included and one on the outside. Otherwise, an orgy. Often bringing pain or relief. Always providing tension. Thin lines of connection, seemingly strong but frequently fragile. Questions: when, why, why not, what now?

Tricornered hat. Three-legged stool. Three-wheeled car.

Triangulation. Surveyor's process. Fixes position of unplotted item in relationship to two known objects. Can also establish distance between two points or position of two points. Relationships implicit.

A musical instrument.

Right. Isosceles. Equilateral. Obtuse. Acute. Scalene. Scalene?

Women readers reading women writers writing women characters righting wrongs.

I have been pondering the relationships among these groups of women from a different perspective recently, having just returned from a well-organized and well-attended East Coast mystery convention filled with writers and readers. During the panel discussion explicitly focused on the subject of gender and also one about cozy novels, and therefore implicitly about gender as most of the readers and writers of this genre nowadays are women, a strong subtext came through. When were women writers with women protagonists going to write novels with male detectives? And how could men be persuaded to read novels by women, about women, or ostensibly for women? As these positions were alternately challenged and defended, I was nagged by a question mystery writers are asked all the time: When are you going to write a real novel? Contemporary mystery writers have learned to recognize that question in all its disguises; and they know the answer. Mystery fiction *is* real fiction. It garners, according to recent statistics, 21 or 22 percent of all sales in the United States; it fills library shelves; it draws buyers to well-stocked sections in bookstores. Yet, the implication of mystery fiction's second-class status is easily supported by our culture. Reviewers, interviewers, newspaper reporters, and television hosts are not

3

embarrassed to ask; often they don't understand how offensive the question is, even when it is pointed out to them.

What then of mystery fiction written by, or about, or for women? Even if one goes back in history no further than the founding days of the genre, in both England and the United States, where mysteries as we now know them were invented, women were second-class citizens. Legally they had almost no rights; economically; they had little power; personally, they were circumscribed and limited. Nonetheless, some were writers: Hawthorne railed against "those damned scribbling women" who interfered with his sales and the Brontës were vilified when they republished their fiction under their own—female—names. And many were readers: then, as now, women were the bulk of fiction readers although the absence of universal literacy frequently excluded working-class and poor women.

And so, why has a genre which finds itself undervalued in the hierarchization process established hierarchies of its own? I would date the beginning of the gender/genre wars at the midpoint in the Golden Age of detective fiction. Although earlier practitioners had included Mary Roberts Rinehart and the sensationalist novelists like Mary Elizabeth Bradden alongside Arthur Conan Doyle and Edgar Allan Poe, the enormous popularity of subsequent women writers such as Agatha Christie, Dorothy L. Sayers, Margery Allingham, and Ngaio Marsh offered a tempting target. The *Black Mask*-ers issued their challenge: gender, genre, nationality. Following a macho credo, they ruthlessly appropriated the dominant culture's icons of masculinity, anti-intellectualism, capitalism, and chauvinism. Hard-boiled fiction was marked off as the domain of men—writers, readers, characters—striding down mean American streets with a gun and a quick left jab. The classical detective novel, they jeered, was no more than a saunter through English villages with lords or little old ladies. A body in the street was worth more points than a body in the library; street smarts outranked Oxford or Cambridge; terse slang topped leisurely conversations; action beat thinking. That the dichotomies were false was irrelevant. An image had been created; and an ex-Pinkerton detective called Hammett walked the walk and talked the talk.

Timing, of course, is never coincidental. The Golden Age and the battle for ownership of the genre immediately followed the first women's movement of the twentieth century and the widespread acceptance (in England and the United States) of women's suffrage. The new debates over women private eyes, the "cozy" mystery, and access to the overwhelmingly female readership began in the midst of the second women's movement. And, the feminist theories of this period—1968 to to the present—provide the tools with which to examine this explicitly gendered connection. In the nineties, there are more women readers reading women writers writing women characters righting wrongs than ever before.

The interpretations of literary texts—a category in which detective fiction would not have been included—during the nineteenth century, when the genre was founded, looked first to the writer for the essential meaning of the text. Biographical criticism was inescapable: who was the writer; when and where did he (or, much less frequently where lit crit was concerned, she) write; what were his politics, religion, nationality; who were his friends, literary ancestors, supporters. From such biographical information, judges of literature often knew before reading the text what it would contain and how best to rank it. The role of the text for someone like Matthew Arnold was to reveal how closely the character of the writer conformed to the moral and ethical standards Arnold and like thinkers had already decided was truth. The reader's only function—and here readers would have been the common herd rather than the judges and arbiters—was to learn the truth and to practice right living. It will surprise no one reading this essay to discover that this method of connecting the writer, the text, and the reader is still in practice today.

When I attended college in the mid-1960s, the then old "new criticism" was still avant-garde on many campuses. In this formulation, the author dropped out of the equation. Biography was not only unstudied but actively dismissed. Anonymous was the preferred author. Meaning, sought by generations of students between the lines, was to be found exclusively within the words on the page. Read correctly, texts provided the same complex meaning semester after semester. I absorbed this lesson so well that when I began teaching full-time in 1973, I fit comfortably into a department where this was the preferred mode of good reading and good teaching.

Among the new theoretical approaches which came to mark the 1970s—a period which introduced theory as a category of literary study with as much validity (and greater employment prospects for graduate students) as Romantic poetry—were reader response and feminist theories. Neither was monolithic: versions of each abounded, making strenuous claims on their adherents. Both had in common a respect for readers, although their arguments grew out of different starting places. Reader response theorists allowed the interpretive power of readers to wander across a spectrum which ranged from complete control and authority to shared status with author and text to critical analysis of clues, patterns, genres, and gaps provided by authors in texts. Feminist critics, on the other hand, began with the underlying premise of respect for women's experiences, authority, opinions—in short, women's readings of life and texts. Persuaded that men had appropriated the privileges of reading and interpretation to themselves, feminist critics asserted not only women's right to interpret the male world but their authority to define the female world. That the early homogeneous definitions of woman soon gave way to a plethora of descriptions of women has reinforced the position of the individual reader as a force to be reckoned with. The two theoretical communities, reader response and feminist, overlap in an important way without ever being subsumed one into the other.

But feminist criticisms also have a vested interest in the writers and their texts. Early analyses focused on revealing the patriarchal messages of male writers and male-focused texts while at the same time activists ransacked the archives for women writers and their texts. Nothing in my experience of twenty-four years as a feminist critic equals the feminist sessions at the 1973 MLA Convention. Relegated to tiny rooms, women sat on top of the furniture and each other, hung in the doorways, and ranged themselves down the halls. These were the places where now-familiar names like Sarah Orne Jewett, Willa Cather, Kate Chopin, Doris Lessing, Dorothy Richardson, and others were first scribbled in dozens of notebooks to make their way onto syllabi back home. For feminists the first vital questions were who wrote; when, where, how, and why she wrote; who or what helped and hindered. When as a group we discovered our lost history—first white, middle-class women, then women of color, working-class women, immigrants, lesbians, non-Europeans, non-contemporary writers—every text mattered deeply. Twenty-some years has not changed that; gynocriticism—attention to the female-authored text—remains a central principle of feminist studies. For feminist theories and literary criticism, the three—writer, text, reader—cannot be separated; they reinforce each other, reverberating at the intersections.

However, it is not sufficient to group the three entities—writers, texts, and readers—in the same time and space, expecting that their connections and intersection are always obvious. The pattern is often described as linear, even when the term is not specifically employed: the writer (#1) composes the text (#2) which is absorbed and understood by the reader (#3). Or sometimes, the reverse: the reader (now #1) absorbs the text (still #2) and understands both the text and the writer (in position #3). Occasionally, the linear is given a circular spin: writer to text to reader to writer to infinity; or reader to text to writer to reader and so on. What each of these one-way methods lacks is an essential feminist element: the opportunity to talk back. These unidirectional analytical methods remind me of the double-file lines of little girls in uniforms so prominent in my Catholic elementary school or of the apocryphal motto of Alaskan sled dogs: unless you are the lead dog, the view never changes. And so, there is a stake in being #1 which is why literary theorists expend so much energy in defending their positions.

Which brings me (you were beginning to wonder?) to triangles. If writer, text, and reader each assume one of the triangle's points, the necessary lines which connect those points obviously run both ways: from point A to point B as well as from point B to point A. And they run from both A and B to point C. If writer and reader are A and B (either can be A; there are no alphabetical hierarchies here), then the line which connects them, like a telephone wire or a fax line, operates in both directions. They influence each other. This leaves point C for the text. The lines which run from both A and B to C are similarly two-way. Reader and writer influence and are influenced by the text without being forced to lose contact with each other. (I hope no one needs a diagram.) I would love to borrow from the dictionary list of types of triangles to call this model a "right" triangle or even an "acute" triangle but common sense and a strong feminist commitment to collaboration have led me to only one accurate term: equilateral triangle. In an equilateral triangle all three angles (the points at which I've positioned the writer, text, and reader) are equal and all three sides (the connecting, two-way lines) are also equal. None dominates; none controls; none waits patiently on the sidelines. Like a three-legged stool, this equilateral triangle of theory is balanced, sturdy, and useful.

Despite this cozy idea of connection among all the elements of the triangle, there is little assurance of a satisfying fit among writer, text, and reader as anyone who has ever thrown down a book in boredom or disgust knows all too well. Such a truth goes a long way toward explaining the prominence of genre categories among books currently being marketed. Genre fiction—westerns, romance, science fiction, fantasy, and mystery fiction—is category marketed because the writer, text, and reader have dependable parameters which the commodifiers seek to honor. Innovation can be hard-fought battle ground. Historically these fictions have been conservative, reinforcing the status quo and supposedly natural behavior. Feminists, in particular, have been eager to reconfigure the models without losing the tremendous popularity and accessibility which the genres represent.

When the three elements of this triangle are preceded by the modifier "mystery"—writer, text, and reader—they take on a precise configuration which distinguishes them from the casual coincidence of any writer and text and reader. The mystery writer, text, and reader are joined together by equal parts of genre, intent, and repetition. Like a successful scientific experiment, genre fiction has to be replicable. The talented author who drops into the field for a one-off may be said to have written a mystery novel but is not a mystery writer. Many texts generously included in an academic syllabus to show the connection of mystery fiction to the broad range of writing can include death, crimes, mysteries, and even detectives without being mystery novels themselves. And the reader of only a single mystery novel may be intrigued, curious and satisfied but cannot truly be labeled a mystery reader.

Genre, as a required element for the writer, text, and reader, is the most difficult to define: how to measure a rubber band? At its most rule-bound, detective fiction as a genre has been marked by proscriptions and caveats. Some of its admittedly best and worst examples have abided by every stricture; others, equally best and worst, have broken rules with ease. And as the puzzle novels of the Golden Age replaced the ratiocinative short stories of the Victorians and were themselves overtaken by the brash American P.I. novels, new sets of rules were added although existing ones were never discarded. As the rubber band expanded, other innovations were tested: police procedurals or women P.I.'s. The genre is now appreciably different from the examples offered by Edgar Allan Poe or Wilkie Collins more than a century ago. Yet the concentrated dialogue among writers and readers about the elements of the text has both revised and reinforced the original and the contemporary shape of the genre.

The careful process by which a writer chooses the pieces of a text makes it unlikely that writing proceeds without intent. And when those choices involve embracing, rejecting, or reconfiguring a known model, the deliberateness involved in creating a text cannot be denied. With reading, however, accidents can happen. One who has no interest in mystery fiction can become intrigued by a single author and read the entire canon; in some cases—Christie, Gardner, Wentworth, etc.—this might prove a formidable library for someone who is not really reading mystery fiction. Travelers read perforce whatever is for sale in otherwise foreign language bookstores, what can be found on shelves left behind by previous visitors, or books traded among groups traveling together; such readers may by accident consume numerous mystery novels without becoming mystery readers. One need not read all varieties of mystery fiction—as there are subgenres, there are subgenre readers—in order to qualify as a mystery reader, but the label does connote voluntary choice, reading within the genre or subgenre, and some awareness that the novels one reads are molded by generic conventions.

The reader's awareness of conventions is, oddly, the characteristic most taken for granted. Contemporary culture, at least in Britain and the United States, deluges the average person with TV cop shows, Sherlock Holmes pubs and T-Shirts, *Murder She Wrote,* movies, newspaper reports, Nancy Drew, and real life—all of which borrow from the mystery genre. My students, who solemnly swear that they have never read a mystery novel (and I believe them), consider themselves sufficiently expert in the genre to reject Barbara Wilson's *Sisters of the Road* as "not a detective novel," although it clearly falls within the boundaries of the genre.

But without immersion in the genre who could write, who could criticize? A writer who tries the genre only once cannot be called a writer of mysteries. As a quick survey of the genre reveals, series have consistently been preferred over singletons. Writers invest themselves in the field through such devices as naming their first book *"A" Is for Alibi* or labeling it A Smith and Wetzon Mystery with all the implied promise of more to come. As the number of awards for Best First Novel by Edgar, Agatha, Anthony, and Shamus committees testify, the field of those who define themselves as mystery writers or readers is actively encouraging new writers to join the group and, by implication, to write a successful second, third, and fourth novel as well. Hence, prizes for Best Novel, Best Paperback Original, Best Private Eye, Best etc. And the message is signaled even more loudly by the repetition of names over the years as writers who have won Best First go on to win subsequent awards. Writing the genre is not, as some who think to earn a quick buck before returning to their real novel believe, a matter of reading half a dozen examples and applying the obvious. Innovation, development, and growth in the genre are a function of those who repeatedly tease the boundaries of the genre, stretch a section of the rubber band, explode a few bombshells, or set an underground mine. They work the familiar unfamiliarly.

Such writers and texts require readers of a similar focus. For all its cultural currency, mystery fiction is not a genre which reveals itself in a single novel. Reading this fiction is, as George Dove proposes, a continuous process of rereading. It assumes what might be called both vertical and horizontal reading. One who knows the history, the genre's past, its prior authors and developments—reading vertically throughout history—knows the tradition in which a writer operates. Horizontal reading takes one laterally through the current scene, meeting writers and texts which are reinforcing existing conventions, challenging prior assumptions, or creating new models. The ideal mystery reader does both. But even those who decline certain strata of the genre to focus, to become expert, to read broadly in their category, deserve the label mystery reader. They are consciously choosing to invest themselves in the genre. Such readers can test each new text against its peers to register, evaluate, accept, or reject developments in the field; in few other fields are so many of the awards for best examples of the work decided by the readers, fans, and consumers. Although I would argue that the genre is not as reader driven as some have claimed, mystery fiction is sustained by a critical mass of authentic mystery readers whose knowledge and acumen make them an integral part of the equation.

When the triangle of writer, text, reader already embellished by the modifier "mystery" is further specified by the gender category "woman," the connections among the three become tighter and the emphasis shifts. As the earlier discussion suggests, the triangulation among the three elements when defined as mystery hums principally along a line which connects reader and writer; it reinforces a pattern whereby the writer and reader negotiate a definition of mystery fiction with which both are satisfied and then produces a text which meets (or challenges) that definition. Although the reader is seldom a singular individual and the text is often a process rather than a product, the genre's grounding in a writer and reader exchange is still a legitimate alliance founded in the desire to produce more mystery texts. The same basic pattern cannot be assumed for the triangle when it expands to include the term "woman"— especially given the nineteenth, early twentieth, and mid-to-late twentieth century women's movements in Britain and the United States, traditional national centers of the mystery genre.

If the term "mystery" applied to writers, texts, and readers establishes a set of expectations, so too does the term "woman." When piled three deep and applied to all points and connections on the triangle in the late twentieth century, it begins to reverberate as "feminist." In so doing, it reinforces a level of expectations and an implied promise similar to the one promised by numerous subtitles in contemporary publishing: "a mystery." In other words, genre fiction is already about expectations; adding another category term—woman, hard-boiled, young adult, historical, etc.—intensifies the focus.

Still, there is no denying that in the current cultural climate, "woman" is a charged term; the ease with which more than one repetition of it in a single utterance can be heard as "feminist" or "women's lib" is easily verifiable. And I contend that even a denial by one of the triangle's components ("I am not a woman writer/reader. My work is not a woman's book. I do not read/write/think/talk/act/publish as a woman.") should first be scrutinized through the lens of contemporary backlash against women, feminism, equality, and power-sharing.

This new triangle turns on the text. It becomes the focal point toward which the writer and reader direct their attention in a gynocritical consideration. The writer may say, "I do or do not write a text which is woman centered," just as the reader may conclude, "I am or am not reading a text which is woman centered." They may agree about the text or disagree. But even if the writer has consciously created her text for a woman reader and a woman reader has made a deliberate choice of works by a woman writer, the binding of that woman-to-woman choice must be found in a woman-centered text; otherwise the connection they establish is based on sex rather than gender.

As any writer, reader, publisher, editor, agent, seller, reviewer, or scholar of mystery fiction in the last quarter of the twentieth century can attest, one of the hallmarks of the contemporary novel is the woman-authored, women-centered text. Of the big five women writers of the Golden Age (Christie, Sayers, Tey, Marsh, and Allingham), only Agatha Christie created women detectives as the protagonists of her novels. Today, the woman detective as protagonist is the overwhelming choice of women writers in a list too long to begin. Their choice of women as main characters at this particular juncture in cultural history—a moment of feminist and equality awareness—and in the midst of a cultural mass of women-centered writing both in the genres and outside has led women mystery writers to produce not simply conventional novels with differently gendered protagonists but gendered novels with noticeably different agendas. These texts have challenged the formula, the conventions, the structure, and the impact of mystery fiction.

Since its beginnings, mystery fiction has valorized gendered texts. Its strong appeal to either rational solutions, painstakingly worked out through clues and logic, or physical action, traded in body blows and gun battles, stresses conventionally ascribed masculine virtues; women were assumed to be both less logical and weaker than men. The abstract appeal to justice in classical novels and the assumption of personal codes of action in the hard-boiled novels similarly approve the lessons taught by society as masculine. Women, as recent feminist psychological studies have demonstrated, are taught to value relationships and interaction over abstractions. And the dominating voice of authority which defines the crime and eventually names the criminal speaks with a singular power denied women even in contemporary society. Finally, the return to order so prized in a classical novel (and even the hard-boiled admission that only the disorder which exists can be preserved) is a glorification of the status quo, a conservative, patriarchal stasis in which the secondary status of women is Edenic only in the Biblical sense.

Contemporary women-centered novels, even those not explicitly called feminist, are using the formula of traditional mystery fiction to trace a new investigation. They overwrite the palimpsest of given conventions without obliterating them completely. In these reworkings, readers can find what might be called archeological strata in layers of revisionist thinking about mystery fiction, women in society, authority, crime, and social justice. The disruption in these novels begins with a striking image: woman as detective as protagonist. The stereotype of the woman detective—the elderly spinster, the naive young woman, the bored housewife—has never been easy to sustain. The contemporary crop of detecting women is not only a critique of those earlier stereotypes and a promise for women's roles in a more open future society but also a challenge to the limitations of women's current roles. Their careers as bounty hunter, criminal attorney, writer, forensics expert, state police officer, business owner, C.P.A., private eye, model, actor, caterer, professor, television personality, computer hacker, park ranger, judge, sheriff, psychiatrist, or journalist may mirror but also exaggerate women's success in breaking into the social power systems.

Thus the impetus for woman as detective as protagonist creates the climate for a woman-centered text. But it also requires a gendered consciousness (which is typically but not always a woman's) as writer and reader to bring the idea to full development. The 1970s and 1980s women private eye novels written by men (and I would contend, for men) prove the best argument: in Arthur Kaplan, Michael Hendricks, and Patrick Buchanan, for example, the woman P.I. is an excuse to titillate readers sexually. The novels are male centered in presenting women as objectifications of sexuality; they are conventionally patriarchal in their dismissive assumptions about women's limited values. The writers are male by sex and gender; the implied readers are gendered male although they may be biologically either male or female.

"Reading like a woman" is a challenge which arose early in the literary criticism of the mid-twentieth century women's movement. Feminists learned from Judith Fetterley how to resist the phallologocentric instructions of contemporary and historical education to read with resistance. As Virginia Woolf had earlier urged that women writers think back through their mothers and write out of the fullness of their female history, so too feminist critics among the reader response theorists began to posit a gendered reading position. Women readers of women writers of women-centered mystery texts follow a similar model in being fully aware of the conventions, traditions, and expectations of the genre while continuously resisting and challenging its basic assumptions. A critical mass of readers who will buy, read, review, praise, and recommend the novels which offer new versions of the mystery is essential to the development of a new strain within the genre. Readers and writers work in conjunction, with a continuous push-pull which encourages and reinforces experimentation, rewards success, and refuses to reject a new focus because of an occasional failure. Gradually the rubber band expands further.

In this woman-oriented trio of writer, detective/text, and reader, the triangle is like a top. It rests on the point of the text in which a woman detective is the locus for a reconsideration of the parameters of the genre. The top is held in motion by the equally weighted positions of the writer and the reader in a balanced contract keeping it spinning upright. If any part of the contract is breached, if any point on the triangle gives way, the whole comes crashing down. In a cultural state where the modifier "woman" is so highly charged—and so open to a negative attack—this brilliantly spinning top is held up by the sheer force of will of its three elements combined in an equilateral equation which requires a leap of faith as each relies on the continuing presence of the other. As the title of this essay suggests in its mathematical allusion, the power of this collaboration—women times women times women—is exponential in its ability to effect revision, growth, and reevaluation in the genre.

A Question of Visibility:
Paretsky and Chicago

Margaret Kinsman

Far away in London, where I have lived for more than twenty years—far away that is from Chicago, from a 1960s suburban Hinsdale adolescence, from my youth, from my American-ness—someone gave me a Sara Paretsky novel, with the off-hand view that I might like it, given my partiality for detective fiction and my American origins. What astonishes me now is that I can't remember which novel it was, who gave it to me, or indeed exactly when, six or seven years ago, it was. It seems as if I had never not read her, never not had access to this refreshing oasis. I fell upon Paretsky's Chicago-located detective novels as a reader not unlike Doris Lessing's exiled Martha, who "read[s] and search[es] with the craving thought, What does this say about my life?" (62).

I recall the discovery of Paretsky, and her investigating protagonist, V.I. Warshawski, coinciding with the invitation to my twenty-fifth high school reunion in Chicago. The emotional landscape would have been ripe for a nostalgia trip—one of those journeys that unleash unresolved puzzles and mysteries in one's own life. But the embedded, informing question is, of course, what *does* V.I.'s life as an achieving, autonomous professional woman in Chicago say to me about my own life?

Most simply, V.I. and her creator make me visible to myself in a multitude of ways. As a reader I reflect and relocate myself in the protagonist, in the writer, in their created structures of meaning and in the city I used to know so well. The personal coherence of V.I.'s Chicago is of particular interest to me because of my remembered city; and because of the notion that real cities furnish material for literary myth as well as for memory. Chicago features prominently here, being both concrete and abstract, a famous place *and* an idea.

But more significantly, Paretsky's literary "maps" of Chicago and the life of an autonomous female appeal to me because of the way in which a single professional woman is authentically and accurately portrayed holding her own in the potentially corrupting milieu of city

15

civic spaces. Obviously, it is high time more of the likes of us were "mapped" in books. As Maggie Humm points out in a recent essay on feminist detective fiction, "The question of who sees what is at the heart of detective fiction" (248).

V.I.'s city of choice, like mine, may well be experienced as a place of indifference, greed, corruption—a jungle, a pit, a monster lacking in anything so decent as an available and affordable parking space. Paradoxically, Chicago and London are also where V.I. and I are empowered to live capable professional and personal lives here at the end of the twentieth century. Making daily sense of *my* city where public space and social restrictions remain in question as far as women are concerned, I recognize many of V.I.'s strategies for dealing with *her* environment.

We bring our own meaning to words. How we do that is mysterious; and mysteries want deciphering. Virginia Woolf theorized that the mystery has to do with appetite; in an early essay on fiction, she wrote that her purpose was "to show the mind at work upon a shelf full of novels and to watch it as it chooses and rejects, making itself a dwelling-place in accordance with its own appetites" (94). What follows is something of a detective story, which has relied on self-interrogation as the principal method of inquiry into the question of what makes Paretsky and V.I. a "dwelling-place" for me.

Examining my current position as a woman reader of Paretsky propelled me briefly into the past to consider my own history of reader-response. Revisiting Jane Addams, I unearthed my dusty edition of her 1895 Hull House Maps and Papers and reflected on this early, if not first, effort in the direction of mapping sociological and demographic characteristics in urban neighborhood districts. Addams established the areas of major study for subsequent decades of Chicago sociologists; and she made an indelible impression on me as a young teen-age suburban reader. Long before I knew anything about sociology or demography, I "saw" and understood Chicago neighborhoods through her story, rooted in a community of women working and achieving together. From Addams the cartographer, I learned something about reading as a traveler. A few years earlier, Nancy Drew, the detecting heroine who always learned something about herself in the course of her investigation, had been providing me with a blueprint for the getting of personal wisdom. Aged eleven and twelve, I couldn't get enough of her. Jane Addams and Nancy Drew rolled into one—no wonder I responded to Paretsky and V.I. with an appetite.

The question of how texts become meaningful brought me eventually, inevitably, to literary theory and feminist scholars. Again,

Virginia Woolf, pondering some fifty years ago on reader-response, wrote, "the reader has in common with the writer, though much more feebly: the desire to create" (94). Contemporary feminist literary theory and crime fiction genre theory are attentive to questions of reader response, reader pleasure, and the complexity of the reading experience. This critical attention to transactions between reader, writer, critic, and protagonist from such theorists as Maggie Humm, Jessica Mann, Carolyn Heilbrun, Dennis Porter, and others provides for me (as reader, researcher, and teacher) spaces with meaning, to borrow Catherine Stimpson's phrase.[1] And the question of the personal pronoun in feminist academic writing further interests me. Nicole Ward Jouve's and Nancy K. Miller's recent works on the autobiographical voice in critical writing, the emergence of the personal in feminist criticism, along with Heilbrun's earlier work on writing women's lives, validate the more personal, flexible idiom to which I am drawn. The writer/scholar in me is recognizable as the women detectives I so enjoy reading. Like them, I collect information; puzzle about connections and links; explore pluralities of meaning; embrace irony, contradiction, discrepancy; tolerate uncertainty; and eventually figure it out. In this particular scenario, *I* feature as the chief investigator, conquering self-doubt in my search for order and the right word.

And finally, the feminist in me is recognizable in the significance of other feminist protagonists, both fictional and real, who have evolved out of generations of feminist politics framed by a profound conviction of the specificity of gender to the systematic social injustices that women suffer across divides of race, class, nationality, sexuality. This results in constant puzzles and problem-solving: of how to be, of what to say, of how to stand up for the self, of what is expected, of how to resist, of how to write a woman's life. Like Paretsky and V.I., I take, not so much for granted, but as the task, the recognition that we speak, read, and write from what Nelly Furman calls "a gender-marked place within our social and cultural context" (52).

At any rate, there I was, far away in London reading Paretsky: thirsty for Chicago and extremely curious about V.I.'s life, where geographic, cultural, and historic specificity are Vic's and her author's constructs, connected to and yet not mine. I found myself in driving need of a map, possessed of a desire to make Chicago visible again while pondering the links between these three constructs of V.I.'s and Paretsky's, and mine. Indirect and complex on one level, on another level the constructs can seem like simple references from one to the other. For instance, in the novel *Toxic Shock*, the Hinsdale that Paretsky constructs of words, was immediately triumphantly irrefutably *my*

Hinsdale . . . an old town about twenty miles west of the Loop whose tall oaks and gracious homes were gradually being accreted by urban sprawl . . . [is] not Chicago's trendiest address, but there's an aura of established self-assurance about the place. Hoping to fit into its genteel atmosphere, I put on a black dress with a full skirt and gold buttons. (65)

While she does not specify V.I.'s destination by street, I am certain as the excited reader that I know exactly where V.I. parks in my town; and I am in no doubt of the significance of bringing my meaning to bear on Paretsky's words.

I want now to turn briefly to a discussion of a literary past in order to frame my subsequent comments on a Paretsky present. Beyond the crime fiction genre, themes of the city and the individual resonate throughout nineteenth- and twentieth-century literatures. The question of autonomy in city streets resonates in particular ways for women, who operate in a world of restraint, where it is the masculine privilege to travel unencumbered and to observe life. The ambiguous double-edged promise of danger and freedom when individual meets city more often frames the narrative of the male protagonist than the female person, as we can see in the Chicago canon.

Constructed primarily by a wave of writers converging in the city in the early 1890s, the Chicago Renaissance laid the groundwork for the received account of Chicago as a mechanical, inhuman, brutalizing environment. Chicago, according to James Hurt in his book *Writing Illinois,* "surely one of the most described, fictionalized, mythologized of cities" (97), is overwhelmingly familiar to us as Sherwood Anderson's "roaring city"; as Sandburg's "hog-butcher for the world"; as Upton Sinclair's "jungle"; as Lincoln Steffens's "first in violence, deepest in dirt; loud, lawless, unlovely." A few decades later, it was Herzog's "clumsy, stinking, tender Chicago"; Algren's "writer's and fighter's town"; Bellow's "somber city"; Mailer's "honest town." Sidney Bremer points to the way in which this male literary tradition "tended to objectify the city as a national concern" contrasting this with what she identifies as a lost counter-tradition of Chicago women writers (Edith Wyatt, Susan Glaspell and many others) dealing with more intimate visions of the city as a base of human action and of organic systems of community—families, neighborhoods, markets, workplaces (Bremer 225).

What seems to be paramount in these less well-known narratives are the themes of *possibility* and *conscience* offered by the city's infinitely rich environment of cultural diversity, rather than the predominant literary vision of a Chicago "given over to male Oedipal conflict." (Bremer 101). Paretsky says significantly of her own first summer in Chicago, 1966, "It was a time of great excitement and hope in the city, and I fell in love with the place—with the bigness and the sense of possibility" (Koch 33). "This was the first place that I'd really been on my own, and I think . . . getting so involved in the city made a permanent impression on me" (Ross 336).

Barbara Berg's study of the origins of American feminism, *The Remembered Gate*, focusing on the woman and the city in the nineteenth century, also draws attention to a female literary counter-tradition. She looks at how, as male and female spheres of activity and influence are increasingly separated in the nineteenth century shift from a largely agrarian existence to the industrial, urban milieu, the requirements of domestic order, especially as a bulwark, a sanctuary against the mean city streets, serve to fetter female energy and activity. Berg points to a nineteenth-century body of fiction by females that defied this orthodoxy, being full of "capable, imaginative and successful urban heroines . . . with confidence in their physical strength and capability . . . infused with vitality, ambition, and initiative" (141). This could, of course, describe V.I. Warshawski. Berg further makes a link between the "literarily expressed craving to find a fulfilled female self" and the subsequent nineteenth-century explosion of "female voluntary associations in cities across the nation" (142).

Chicago at the turn of the twentieth century provided an impressive example of effective networks of women using their energies outside the home, sharing experiences and collective action across divisions of age, class, and culture in the face of urban poverty, illiteracy, and exploitation. Women became visible and mobilized in an urban public sphere demonized in print as greedy, threatening, cut-throat. Their stories demonstrate, like Jane Addams's story of Hull House, a city beginning to accept the force of female energy. In the same vein, Liz Heron's recent anthology *Streets of Desire*

looks to the city as the site of women's most transgressive and subversive fictions throughout the century, as a place where . . . constraints can be cast off and new freedoms explored. . . . City fictions are often narratives of self-discovery . . . seem[ing] to insist on the autonomous status of female experience . . . [the place] where women come into their own. (2-3)

Again, the link with Paretsky and her own experience of Chicago seems clear. In a 1988 interview, Paretsky said, "I think I was very fortunate that I was in my early twenties when the women's movement came alive in Chicago" (Ross 336).

Paretsky's portrayal of Chicago reveals her own experience and understanding of its geography, politics, people, and problems. Tillie Olsen in *Silences* identifies a "characteristic strain" in women's fiction as being a "concern with wrongs to human beings" (42). The crime fiction genre obviously lends itself to expressing concern with wrongdoing, and in Paretsky's hands links us to the Chicago literary legacy of women writers celebrating female characters of depth, ingenuity, intellect, energy. Kathleen Gregory Klein describes Paretsky's novels as "dense with the atmosphere of Chicago [and] a single woman's life amidst friends and family" (830). This junction, where city and a woman's life in it intersect, is the critical one for me, in both personal and literary terms. In reflecting on this notion of visibility—that is, how a city and the life of a contemporary woman are rendered literally and metaphorically visible in the Paretsky oeuvre, I was struck by the extent to which the writer draws on two recurrent motifs in the crime fiction genre (as well as in your and my life)—the car and the restaurant—as metaphors for V.I.'s independence, for the "knowability" of her community, for her mobility, and for her social participation in the city. Certainly my own vehicle and the public spaces of London restaurants that I know and frequent are both significant features of life as I live it; and both are linked to the meanings I see in the novels.

Before taking a closer look at cars and restaurants in V.I.'s Chicago, I want to speculate about maps and their significance in relation to visibility. Maps, like cities, imply the possibility of choices: losing the way, rather than gaining the way, is always possible. We gaze at maps, flat and representing objective direction, in order to be guided to a location. Topography, satisfactory for at least the two dimensions of latitude and longitude, scarcely accommodates the third, or any other, dimension. The map—an object known for its utility in getting us from one place to another—is the intermediary surface between the state of the wanderer and the traveler. Maps require continual updating.

Chicago has been as famously mapped by the urban sociologists as it has been written about. Carla Cappetti's highly original study of the relationships between the urban sociologists and the novelists of 1920s and 1930s Chicago includes a fascinating chapter on "Maps, Models and Metaphors." She argues, "If maps are a main vehicle for imposing order on what appears to the outside as chaos, words are another of at least equal importance" (54-55). Maps make order visible. Detectives and researchers make order visible. Liz Heron expresses something similar to Cappetti when she writes that "the ease or difficulty with which the spaces of the city are negotiated plays out the symbolic drama of women's visibility or invisibility. In this plotting of mobility, women's cultural and social status is explored" (5-6). It is Heron's "plotting of mobility" I want next to explore in relation to V.I., who, in a perpetual motion of discovery, never seems to refer to the sort of map you pull out of the glove compartment.

V.I. steers by memory, instinct, dream, conviction, history—using these as if they were maps of those other dimensions, distances past and future, that are not found in the folds of the Rand-McNally. Paretsky reveals a great deal of V.I.'s value system through an extended urban iconography (much of which Vic comments on from the perspective of her car) making both the city and V.I.'s relationship to it visible.

One of the ways the car functions in the novels is to express V.I.'s powerful sense of direction. As she drives around the greater Chicago area, she provides a topography of the road and a clear indication that she knows exactly where she is going. Her quests around the city are successful on several levels. First, she gets to where she is going and returns, overcoming or circumventing obstacles en route. "I never get lost driving in Chicago," she says in *Bitter Medicine*. "If I can't find the lake or the Sears Tower, the L tracks orient me, and if all else fails, the x-y street coordinates keep me on target" (23).

More symbolically, she usually finds or learns something in the course of her urban journeys that aids her search for truth, while helping the reader make sense both of the texture of her life and of the moral landscape she occupies in her mean city streets. V.I.'s fondness for the underdog, for example, is implied by her thoughts about the Cubs baseball team as she cruises past Wrigley Field or listens to the game on the car radio. She frequently muses on the Cubs who, in *Indemnity Only*, "had bad days, too—in fact more than I did probably" (112). Given a spare hour or two, her support for the basically no-hope team often takes her as an active spectator to the ballpark to cheer them on.

Other clues to her value-system are revealed in her resistance to received opinion on famous Chicago architectural triumphs. Moving around the commercial streets of the Chicago Loop in *Bitter Medicine*, Vic shows no respect for convention as she skeptically notes to herself:

My friends and I have financed one of the worst monstrosities known to woman on the northwest corner of the Loop. . . . Designed by Helmut Jahn, it is a skyscraper made of two concentric glass rings. . . . we get to pay heat and cool a place that is mostly open space. Still, it won an architectural award in 1986, which I guess proves how much the critics know. (163)

V.I.'s consistent and concrete sense of direction as a driver and a traveler in her city helps me understand and accept the similar purposefulness she expresses and develops in relation to her own life. Greatly valuing the choices she makes about career, marital status, place of residence, friendships, V.I. has elected to remain a single woman, to remain in the city, and to engage in urban adventures. Rare bouts of bewilderment about the direction of her life are expressed primarily in her dreams, where she lets go of the logic and reason required in her daily professional world. The opening of *Burn Marks* offers the profoundly personal topography of a dream, representing part of the ongoing process of Vic's self-identification in confronting her past:

My mother and I were trapped in her bedroom, the tiny upstairs room of our . . . old house on Houston. Down below the dogs barked and snapped as they hunted us. Gabriella had fled the fascists of her native Italy but they tracked . . . her all the way to South Chicago. . . . I sat up. It was three in the morning. . . . I was sweaty and trembling from the dream's insistent realism. (1)

Paretsky thus turns tradition upside down. Taking the familiar landscapes of Chicago, of a hard-boiled detective novel, and of a woman's life, the writer treats them as fluid/in flux, requiring us to "see" them differently. The precision of Paretsky's efforts to map V.I.'s city and her P.I. life on its streets is linked to the cartographer's task of visualizing and charting. This in turn is related to the considerable confusion the observer (whether mapmaker, writer, sociologist, or detective) is dealing with. The crime fiction genre is imbued with the same impulse to observe potential menace and threat, to order what is chaotic into a familiar pattern of cause and consequence, to tame the disorder. Above all to explain—to banish ambivalence and contradiction. P.D. James reminds us, in a 1986 *Newsweek* interview, "Detective stories help reassure us in the belief that the universe, underneath it all, is rational. They're small celebrations of order and reason in an increasingly disordered world" (83).

The detective, high celebrant of order and reason, is in charge of the ritual. When the detective herself poses the threat of disorder, as V.I. does to policeman Bobby Mallory's sense of what constitutes an appropriate life for a woman, and to various lovers whose sense of propriety leads them to try to protect Vic, then the narrative task of representing a return to order is complicated by the necessity to represent simultaneously the departure from order. Vic, the competent and capable protagonist dealing with her share of both the risk and the excitement the city offers to women, arouses incomprehension and disapproval from some and affirmation from others, her place in the text as a single, achieving, avowedly feminist P.I. already signifying visible disorder.

Now, the mythology of mean city streets and the detective who operates/eats alone both have a strong purchase in the crime fiction genre, particularly in the private-investigator tradition. "Mean city streets" brings to mind, as the phrase is meant to, configurations of murder, fear, betrayal, danger. It also brings to mind the individual, lone, and heroic fight for justice waged by the detective protagonist. Mean city streets provide the moral landscape against which the crusade takes place, and the reader sees them through the crusader's eyes. The complex representation of V.I.'s private-investigator life on Chicago's streets is elaborated to a significant extent, as I indicated earlier, by Paretsky's treatment of two urban P.I. images—the car and the restaurant.

The ordinary car and the ordinary event of eating alone in public operate as powerful symbols of V.I.'s refusal to countenance that there might be places where she cannot or "should not" go. While her car literally takes her to places where she is not supposed to be, snooping around factories, warehouses, loading docks, building sites, other people's office buildings, the car also signals figurative places she occupies. First, the car simultaneously establishes her individuality in a society obsessed with cars and setting great store by the latest model; and it locates her firmly in the P.I. tradition where the detective drives an oddball car—foreign, or bashed up, or distinctively sporty. Here, V.I.'s old Chevy and, subsequently, her beloved Trans Am distinguish her. Next, the car authenticates her as an achieving professional woman with the means to buy and maintain her own status symbol, reminding me of the change in some of the economic and social constraints historically characteristic of women's lives. The car has been a great leveler for women in the twentieth century; this literal mobility has accompanied— even generated—social and personal possibilities for females. V.I. belting up the expressway pushing 80 mph in her Chevy is no different at that point from Detective Rawlings speeding at the wheel of his Buick.

Third, the car stands as a symbol of Vic's energizing desire for the truth and for her autonomy, which she occasionally needs to distinguish from the more fleeting desire she might feel for the likes of the flashy '86 Nissan Maxima driven by the corrupt Dr. Burgoyne in *Bitter Medicine*: "If I'd gone into corporate law and kept my mouth shut when I was supposed to, I'd be driving a car like this. . . . You can't have everything in this life" (75). And finally, the car is a device (somewhat like the traditional sleuth's sidekick) for signaling V.I.'s keen observational powers and potency as a witness. While she drives, she conducts a running commentary of sorts on Chicago, at the same time bringing her observational skills to bear on a dialogue about the city and herself. The opening pages of *Toxic Shock* find V.I. meditating on a return to the South Chicago of her childhood:

I had forgotten the smell. Even with the South Works on strike and Wisconsin Steel padlocked and rusting away, a pungent mix of chemicals streamed in through the engine vents. I turned off the car heater, but the stench—you couldn't call it air—slid through minute cracks in the Chevy's windows, burning my eyes and sinuses. (11)

In much the same way that V.I.'s legendary powers of navigation are both explicitly and implicitly signaled by the car motif, so does her encyclopedic knowledge of where to eat en route function as a signifier. V.I.'s ability to locate an eating establishment in almost any neighborhood, enter it with self-possession, and then benefit from the rewards of the subsequent nourishment (food, information, thinking time, rest, whatever) is, I suggest, like the car, an effective and particular means to the end of portraying her as simultaneously "outside" the convention and as having a persistent concern with the nature of locale and community. In *Guardian Angel*, fed up with dense traffic heading north on Halsted, V.I. gets off "at Jackson where the remnants of Chicago's Greek community lie . . . [and settles] down with taramasalata and a plate of grilled squid" (130). A woman eating alone in public might be marked as eccentric, deranged, or "failed." But V.I.'s solitary public eating and drinking signals this as a normal, knowable activity— an acceptable alternative to the private space of hearth, kitchen, and family to which women are traditionally confined. Eating out demonstrates V.I.'s vast store of information about her city and her social mobility; she knows where to go. It also establishes her economic credentials. She eats fairly modestly and not regularly, but with deep appreciation of the values of hard work and good cooking. Eating out with Lotty at their favorite haunt, the Dortmunder Hotel, Vic reflects on both her food and her friend:

I hadn't eaten much of the cottage-cheese plate in the deli at lunch so I indulged myself with a veal chop and the special potatoes the Dortmunder makes, double-fried so they're crisp on the outside and soft and fluffy inside. Lotty ordered a seafood salad and coffee. But then, she's smaller than I am; she burns fewer calories. Or so I rationalized. (*Bitter Medicine* 178)

Often too hard up for the new pair of Nikes she could use, Vic, the daughter of working-class parents, is thrifty, but self-reliant, and able to nourish herself. Finally, the motif of eating alone in public establishes V.I. in an information and support network consisting largely of women—bartenders, waitresses, chefs, owners, upon whom Vic is sometimes reliant for sustenance and protection, as when Barbara and Helen of the Belmont Diner rather effectively foil one of V.I.'s pursuers with a jug of iced tea in *Guardian Angel*. While this sisterhood remains somewhat more anonymous to readers than the immediate community of Lotty and Co., it nevertheless contains other role models of independent achieving women such as the redoubtable Sal, owner of Vic's favorite Loop bar, The Golden Glow. Sal's business skills are given credit by V.I. in *Bitter Medicine*:

Sal was sitting behind the horseshoe mahogany bar when I came in, reading *The Wall Street Journal*. She takes her investments seriously, which is why she spends so much time in the bar when she could retire to the country. Sal tops my five eight by a good four inches and has a regal bearing to match. No one behaves in an unseemly fashion at the Golden Glow when Sal is there. (174)

These snapshots of other women characters give the reader more evidence of the possibilities this city of Chicago holds (and by extension other contemporary cities) for female empowerment, autonomy, and sisterhood. V.I.'s vision of Chicago, explicitly and implicitly shared with most of her female friends and allies, is consistently informed by her abiding awareness of gender, race, and class; together, these women understand how such factors, historically and contemporaneously, shape and affect them in their city. Understanding the city as a racially and economically diverse and *divided* society, Vic inhabits and traverses a physical and moral landscape she is utterly familiar with and far from complacent about.

Detective novels traditionally emphasize the safety of such stable boundaries as geography, class, race, and gender. However, Paretsky's narratives disrupt the stability of this legacy by moving the boundaries, by transgressing divides, by opening up lines of communication (verbal equivalents of roads, ferries, bridges, railway tracks, rivers, canals) that did not exist before, as Vic drives and eats her way around Chicago. Her Chicago is a turbulent one—indeed the streets are full of pursuers, ambush, violence, cynicism—to which she is persistently alert. Lives can be lived and lost in the city and never missed at all. The stories of the aging and isolated Mitch and Mrs. Frizzell (both of whom die from a combination of human neglect and greed in *Guardian Angel*) spring to mind as prime Paretsky examples of society's dangerous and ominous tendency to treat whole sections of itself as disposable. But V.I.'s city is also a network of extended family and friends reaching from Max on the North Side through Lotty's less than fashionable Irving Park neighborhood to V.I.'s roots in South Chicago. Her ability to traverse all of these in a day, in a memory, in an observation, in a car, knits together a web of connection, support, mutual responsibility, information-sharing, collaborative action. Thus Paretsky echoes the counter-tradition of Chicago women's novels to which I referred earlier, sharing the resistance to impositions of gender, genre, and canon. The car and the restaurant carry meaning for V.I.'s participation in and independence of the community, as well as her resistance to the constraints of convention. Like the Chicago literary sisters before her, Paretsky's continuing stories of V.I. and her city demonstrate a profound understanding of the notions that in a world as divisive as our urban ones are, connection with a highly visible female community is something to cherish; and tales of conscience and a woman's concerns with wrongdoing are of value.

And now, a denouement of sorts. In a 1991 article in *Ms.* magazine, Carolyn Heilbrun, aka Amanda Cross, wrote: "Women are natural detectives, catching signs, intuiting connections, bravely confronting a recalcitrant and malevolent society and the men whom it serves" (64). This particular detective story of mine, related in the venerable tradition of the informal essay, has, as yet, an unresolved ending. Like any good mystery lover, and like many feminist "natural detectives," I have a highly developed tolerance for ambiguity, for shifting boundaries, for irresolution. But that is as it should be at the moment. I have tried to explain only the significance of a certain train of thought in relation to some clues about recognition and pleasure, like trying to explain the complex imagery of a photograph—our view of what is in the photograph informed by the triangle of the negative, the print, and our own gaze. The desire for an ending—for mysteries do like a solution—is still somewhat baffled. I am left, and leave you, in the pleasurable state of suspense—of not knowing the outcome even in the process of approaching it. Who knows what V.I., Paretsky, and I and our appetites will be like in our fifties?

Note

1. In the introduction to her 1988 book *Where the Meanings Are*, Catherine Stimpson writes, "So questing, so questioning, I have found feminism a space where meanings are" (xii).

Works Cited

Berg, Barbara J. *The Remembered Gate: Origins of American Feminism, The Woman and the City.* New York: Oxford UP, 1978.

Bremer, Sidney. "Willa Cather's Lost Chicago Sisters." *Women Writers and the City.* Ed. Susan Merrill Squier. Knoxville: U of Tennessee P, 1984. 210-28.

Cappetti, Carla. *Writing Chicago: Modernism, Ethnography and the Novel.* New York: Columbia UP, 1993.

Furman, Nelly. "Textual Feminism." *Women and Language in Literature and Society.* Ed. Sally McConnell, Ruth Borker, and Nelly Furman. New York: Praeger, 1980. 45-54.

Heilbrun, Carolyn G. "The Women of Mystery." *Ms.* 1.5 (1988): 62-64.

Heron, Liz, ed. *Streets of Desire.* London: Virago, 1993.

Humm, Maggie. *Border Traffic: Strategies of Contemporary Women Writers.* Manchester: Manchester UP, 1991.

Hurt, James. *Writing Illinois: The Prairie, Lincoln and Chicago.* Chicago: U of Illinois P, 1992.

Klein, Kathleen Gregory. Sara Paretsky entry in *Twentieth Century Crime and Mystery Writers.* Ed. Lesley Henderson. Chicago and London: St. James, 1991. 830.

Koch, John. "Mystery Woman." *Boston Globe* 5 Feb. 1992: 33, 40.

Lehman, David, with Tony Clifton in London. "A Queen of Crime." *Newsweek* 20 Oct. 1986: 81, 83.

Lessing, Doris. *A Proper Marriage.* London: Panther, 1966.

Olsen, Tillie. *Silences.* London: Virago, 1978.

Paretsky, Sara. *Indemnity Only.* London: Penguin, 1982.

——. *Toxic Shock* (first published as *Bloodshot,* 1988). London: Penguin, 1990.

——. *Bitter Medicine.* New York: Ballantine, 1988.

——. *Guardian Angel.* New York: Delacorte, 1992.

Porter, Dennis. *The Pursuit of Crime: Art and Ideology in Detective Fiction.* New Haven: Yale UP, 1981.

Ross, Jean W. Interview with Sara Paretsky, 6/2/88. *Contemporary Authors.* Ed. Susan M. Trosky. Vol. 129. Detroit, MI: Gale Research, 1990. 334-38.

Stimpson, Catherine R. *Where the Meanings Are.* London: Routledge, 1988.

Woolf, Virginia. "Phases of Fiction." *Granite and Rainbow.* London: Hogarth, 1960. 93-145.

Joan Hess/Joan Hadley:
Separating the Voices

Mary Jean DeMarr

Let's begin with three quotations from critics and writers who have been crucial for feminist and academic women of the last twenty years, then with a generalization which is also a cliche, and finally with a personal parable. These will, I hope, set the stage for a consideration of the detective fiction of Joan Hess, a writer who speaks for and to many women of our time. First, the quotations. Dale Spender comments on the importance of writing to women's culture:

Indeed, there is much evidence that suggests reading (and writing) are at the core of women's culture (in much the same way that football can be said to be at the core of men's culture), but because so much of women's experience has been "invisiblised" this aspect of women's existence attracts little research attention or social validation. So central, however, is reading to feminist reality that it is not unusual to find women acknowledging that a particular book "changed my life"; and so central is writing to feminist experience that it is not unusual to find a feminist defined as "a woman who writes" (this was one version that was put forward at the Women in Publishing Conference, London, November 1985). (46-47)

Adrienne Rich, writing from the perspective of a highly regarded feminist poet, discusses the hegemony of masculine requirements over the needs of both women writers and women readers, but she also hopefully predicts a time when women will be freed of this cultural control:

No male writer has written primarily or even largely for women, or with the sense of women's criticism as a consideration when he chooses his materials, his themes, his language. But to a lesser or greater extent every woman writer has written for men, even when, like Virginia Woolf, she was supposed to be addressing women. If we have come to the point when this balance might begin to change, when women can stop being haunted, not only by "convention and propriety" but by internalized fears of being and saying themselves, then it is an extraordinary moment for the woman writer—and reader. (37-38)

And finally, Judith Fetterley, from the point of view of a feminist critic, discusses the politics of power in the literary canon:

Power is the issue in the politics of literature, as it is in the politics of anything else. To be excluded from a literature that claims to define one's identity is to experience a peculiar form of powerlessness—not simply the powerlessness which derives from not seeing one's experience articulated, clarified, and legitimized in art, but more significantly the powerlessness which results from the endless division of self against self, the consequence of the invocation to identify as male while being reminded that to be male—to be universal, to be American—is to be *not female*. (xiii)

Now the trite generalization and then the personal parable. For many women—and not only academics—feminist criticism of the last twenty years or so has been enlightening and empowering. It has liberated us from a societally imposed alienation and allowed us to set literature which speaks about us and directly to us at the heart of our female culture. To speak personally—and feeling free to speak personally in academic writing is another great gift of feminist criticism and scholarship—it was only when I finally became able to value women's writing about women and women's issues that I felt a true emotional connection to the literature I studied.

As a high school pupil in the late 1940s, a college undergraduate English major in the early 1950s, and a graduate student in English in the late 1950s and early 1960s, I read a completely traditional (that is, masculine) canon. As far as I can remember, through the end of my undergraduate career, the only woman writer assigned in any of my classes was Emily Dickinson. And she was not approached as a woman except insofar as her being both female and a good writer was perceived as an oddity. I read works about women, of course—*The Scarlet Letter* and *Tess of the D'Urbervilles* stand out in my memory—but I read primarily about men, and so, as Fetterley later pointed out, I was trained to "identify as male" (xii). Works like *The Adventures of Huckleberry Finn* and *Moby Dick* were taught as presenting microcosms or universal experiences. And being a docile student, I accepted these generalizations. But I did not find those works truly meaningful to me, and I did not realize that they probably carried much more meaning to my male classmates. Gradually, however, I began reading more and more fiction by women writers, and I took a pleasure and found a meaning in this literature which I discovered on my own that was far more personal and powerful than in my assigned reading. But I was slightly ashamed of my extracurricular reading. Hearing women writers belittled by my teachers and professors, when they were mentioned at all, and being so docile, I assumed that my enjoyment of these writers was simply one more evidence of my undeveloped taste—in addition, of course, to my low taste for detective fiction—though the only female writers in that genre which I can recall reading or even being aware of were Agatha Christie and Ngaio Marsh. I suspect that at the time I considered both types of reading, women writers and mysteries, not quite respectable, and uniting them by seeking out women writers of detective fiction simply never occurred to me.

It was in the late 1950s when I was one of a group of bright women in a graduate seminar on Hemingway that I had my first insight into what was happening. We women students talked to each other about our discomfort with much of what we were reading in Hemingway and his critics, and we began together to formulate our own interpretations and evaluations. True, there existed some published negative critical commentary on Hemingway's women which stimulated and encouraged our evaluations and conclusions, but somehow I think we felt rather daring for questioning the perceptions of a "great" writer. And we had probably no idea that what we were doing was feminist criticism. But it was—and for several of us, at least—it was the beginning of a long journey.

For me, that seminar began the process of connecting to literature, of realizing emotionally as well as intellectually that literature matters, that it can speak to readers about their lives, that it can move them in truly meaningful ways. Indirectly, I think, it began to allow me to value and respect the work of the women writers I had been rather shamefacedly reading and enjoying. I suspect that it led me to an early critical decision—made quite unconsciously—of which I am now proud: in my dissertation, on contributions to American literature by Russian-Jewish and Russian writers, a comparatively large amount of space is given to female writers. Admittedly, none of them was allotted a complete chapter (I rather doubt that I would have been able to convince my dissertation director to allow that—but I also must admit that I didn't think to try to persuade him). In my long introductory and historical chapter, sympathetic examinations are given to such diverse writers as Elizabeth Hasanovitz, Rose Cohen, Mary Antin, Emma Goldman, Anzia Yesierska, Ayn Rand, Nina Fedorova, and others. My arguments there are not by any means feminist, but they clearly place these women into the mainstream of their ethnic groups and favorably explicate their literary works and evaluate their worth, emphasizing the importance of women and women's experience within the Russian-Jewish and Russian immigrant communities.

All this would not be worth recounting were my story not typical of the experience of many women of my generation. It is a lengthy prelude to an examination of a contemporary mystery writer. But it will, I hope, be helpful, as it foregrounds much of what Joan Hess does in her detective novels as well as the way in which her novels may be read by women, including of course feminists, of the 1990s. Hess is one of Spender's "women who write," who "give voice to a different reality," as called for by Fetterley in 1978 (xi).

Although there is a long tradition of female practitioners in the field of mystery and detective fiction—as far back as Anna Katharine Green in the nineteenth century and with such universally acknowledged leading twentieth-century practitioners as Agatha Christie and Dorothy L. Sayers, the explosion of fine female mystery writers in the last fifteen years or so and the ways in which some of these writers have been pressing the genre to—and even beyond—its previously understood boundaries (Ruth Rendell and Sara Paretsky, for example) has infused the entire field with a new energy and has attracted the attention of a broad audience of women readers and critics. Many, though not all, of those new writers appeal especially to the feminist reader because of their own feminist attitudes and assumptions and their sensitive depictions of women's lives and concerns. Many allow female characters to speak forcefully for themselves in new and stimulating ways, most effectively, of course, when like Joan Hess they do not put doctrinaire feminist views in the mouths of their protagonists.

These observations find particularly interesting illustrations in Hess's detective fiction. Her two principal series, both set in the author's native Arkansas, appeal to readers in differing ways because of the differences between them in theme, point of view, setting, tone, situation of central character, number and type of continuing characters, and so on. Crucial here are the differences in protagonist and narrative method, though the two series may be most quickly differentiated by setting. The first series, with Claire Malloy as protagonist, is set in and around Farberville, Arkansas, a college town apparently loosely modeled after the real Fayetteville where Hess lives. Claire's situation as single mother who must of necessity work outside the home is emblematic for our times and speaks to many female readers. The novels, completely told in her first-person point of view, are literate and allusive; they are also concerned with typical issues of contemporary middle-class life, told in a wryly ironic tone by a strong woman confronting problems characteristic of many other women today.

In contrast, Hess's other series under her own name is set in the village of Maggody, Arkansas, and is broadly farcical. Arly Hanks is the police chief of her home town, which sometimes seems like a cross between one of Faulkner's more decadent settings and Erskine Caldwell's primitive locales—but presented in an almost purely comic tone. Arly is out of place in her town. Educated, the survivor of a now-broken marriage and a lengthy sojourn in Manhattan, she can see Maggody both as an insider with intimate knowledge of its convoluted relationships and perversions and as an outsider who is able to comment objectively on these idiosyncrasies. An interesting and unusual mixed point of view is used in these novels: passages told by Arly are interspersed with sections narrated in an omniscient third-person perspective. Here we see a strong woman in a nontraditional profession managing by force of character and personality to accomplish her work; she manages to survive and even flourish in a situation which is far from ideal by dint of her strong sense of humor and ability to see herself and her surroundings objectively.

Claire's Farberville novels would seem to be the more directly aimed at feminist readers of detective fiction; both themes and first-person narrative methods are significant here. Arly's Maggody books might appear to have a somewhat broader appeal, because of their greater concentration on broad comedy and satire; however, the very breadth of the farce is not to all readers' tastes. Her presentation as a woman, moreover, is less full and complex than is Claire's, and the appeal of her series is less focused on women's issues. Thus her novels are of less direct appeal to feminist readers, despite their sympathetic portrayal of the strong central female character and the interest of their mixed point of view.

Hess's third series, published under the pseudonym of Joan Hadley, is even less directly aimed at women readers. The Theo Bloomer books, one set in the Caribbean and one in Israel, with their masculine protagonist and third-person perspective, appear calculated to have the broadest audience appeal of all but are less well known—less successful, in fact—largely because of this very broadening of scope and concomitant lessening of focus upon a particular readership. Outside the scope of this book because of their use of a male detective, this series seems to have been dropped by its writer after only two novels, nothing having been published about Theo Bloomer since 1988.

Voice and characterization, then, are the primary factors in creating a particular appeal to female readers in much of Hess's detective fiction. The series centering on Claire Malloy makes particularly strong use of these two elements. The novels are presented entirely in Claire's voice, a vivid and ironic first-person narrative style. Claire is a widow, supporting herself and her teenaged daughter, adequately if not particularly comfortably, by running a bookstore. Her husband, a professor of English at Farber College, a "provincial liberal arts college" (*Strangled* 9), had been killed in an automobile accident, leaving her to cope alone. She is thirty-eight at the beginning of *Strangled Prose,* the novel in which she is introduced, and Caron, her daughter, is fourteen. Like Arly Hanks in the Ozarks series, when her marriage is ended, she of necessity discovers resources within herself which she did not know she had. Her marriage had appeared outwardly to be a good one, and she seems to the community to represent those women who follow the path socially prescribed for middle-class women, that of homemaking and child-rearing and of self-abnegation; like so many others, she had appeared to be successful in that path until a meaningless tragedy destroyed her emotional and financial security.

She has coped well. When her series begins, eight years have passed since her husband's death, and she has built a new life for herself and her daughter, a life in which she is comfortable and content. At the opening of *Strangled Prose* (which may be relied on to exemplify the characteristics of the series, for the other novels are strikingly consistent with it in characterization and tone), she is in her cramped office, struggling with her ledgers and resisting the temptation to read one of the books on her shelves. In fact, she loves what she does, and her comment on her relationship with the store draws a significant comparison with marriage, indicating her awareness, doubtless as a direct result of her experience, of the fragility of all human connections: "Now [the store] is mine, and like a marriage, the relationship is not dependable. But I love the musty corners, the flaking plaster, and the memories of a happier time. I have always known that I ought to own a bookstore, if only to have access to a satisfactory source of books" (1-2). It quickly becomes clear that she has come to terms with her husband's death and found satisfaction if not gratification in her new independence. In this, she must strike a responsive chord in many female readers of the 1980s and 1990s.

The fragility of relationships and the dangers of middle-class women's placing too much reliance on them is dramatically illustrated by Claire's experience. In addition to causing the loss of her husband and her financial security, however, his fatal accident revealed to her that her trust in him had been misplaced: a young woman had been with him in the car, and thus the existence of his secret life was revealed to her. This fact was hushed up at the time, so Claire carried the burden and pain of her knowledge alone for eight years, both protecting her late husband's reputation and shielding her daughter from knowledge of his perfidy. *Strangled Prose* turns on revelations of shameful information about three members of the Farber College English Department (Claire's husband and two others), and Claire's betrayal is made public, forcing her to defend herself from becoming a possible murder suspect and to deal with her daughter's disillusionment and anger about her father's infidelity. With humor and determination Claire leaps into detecting, in the process evoking a fictional presence of great resonance to generations of women mystery readers by frequently and ironically comparing herself to Nancy Drew.

An important continuing character in all of the novels and an important relationship in Claire's life is Lt. Peter Rosen of the Farberville CID. He is introduced in *Strangled Prose* and plays a significant role in other novels (though occasionally offstage). They strike sparks from the beginning, though it is not always clear whether those are from antagonism or attraction. Indeed, a combination of rivalry and affection characterizes their connection as their intimacy grows. Claire repeatedly becomes involved in mysteries, and Peter regularly urges her to leave the detecting to him, the professional. She in turn feels the need to prove to him that she can on her own extricate herself from difficulty and figure out the solution to crimes. She will not become a damsel in need of being rescued by her lover.

Their relationship seems characteristic of the 1980s and 1990s. Both have survived marriages gone bad: Peter is divorced and generally resists discussing his earlier experience. That it was a painful time for him is evident. Claire knows that her trust in her husband had been misplaced, although she had long concealed that fact; thus she has the added embarrassment of being not only the betrayed wife but also a widow who has lived a polite lie for eight years. Both Peter and Claire are, when they meet, far enough from the end of their marriages to be ready for new involvements. In fact, when readers first meet Claire, she is carrying on an apparently rather halfhearted affair with one of her late husband's colleagues, another aspect of her representative nature as a woman of the 1980s.

Claire's and Peter's relationship is particularly symptomatic of the times in that both are free and mature adults, each with an established lifestyle, a profession, and interests. Claire appears to know almost from the beginning that she is intensely attracted to him (why else would she allow herself to be driven to transparent stratagems to discover whether he is married?), but both her comfort in her independence and her pride impel her to keep Peter at arm's length. And their rivalry as detectives complicates matters.

Though not much is made of Peter's background, it sets him apart and adds to his interest as a character. Claire is an insider in her college community; she knows nearly everybody and nearly everything about everybody, and her connections enable her to find out what she does not already know. Peter, however, who speaks with an alien (Eastern) accent, upsets her stereotypes of small-town Arkansas police:

[He] had curly black hair, a beakish nose, and guileless brown eyes. He wore a well-cut three-piece suit and a discreet tie, as though he had dashed away from his executive suite to tidy up the situation. He lacked a briefcase, but the image was otherwise perfect. My idea of a Farberville cop included a polyester jacket, an undulating midriff, and a perpetual sneer; this contradiction rather surprised me. (*Strangled* 55)

As novel succeeds novel in the series, Claire's and Peter's relationship deepens, and marriage seems a possible result, though in the latest novel, *Death by the Light of the Moon,* Claire is still resisting. Clearly, however, when they are apart she misses him, and she repeatedly calls him from Louisiana to consult him about the weird situation and grotesque murder into which she has become immersed on her visit to her late husband's eccentric mother and family.

One of the most appealing aspects of the series generally is its depiction of the relationship of most importance to Claire as a contemporary woman, that with her daughter. As a mother, she is generally exemplary—caring, steady, firm, objective, and above all with a sense of humor about her daughter and their relationship. Caron is at a particularly trying age—full of melodrama, seeing the world in capital letters and exclamation points, intense in everything she does, fickle in her interests and enthusiasms. Her impatience with her mother and her embarrassment at her mother's behavior must surely be all too familiar to parents of teenagers. When Caron learns of her father's behavior from a thinly veiled depiction in a romance novel *a clef,* Claire knows she must discuss it with her but is hindered by the need to defend herself and by Caron's avoidance of the issue. Caron's new pain and anger are conveyed indirectly, through her mother's ironically detached narrative and through her behavior; the situation adds to the tensions already present between mother and pubescent daughter.

Caron grows older as the series progresses, but she remains an irritating and amusing exemplar of the genus teenager. She and her best friend, Inez Brandon, are inseparable, and their antics and enthusiasms as well as their scorn for the adult world represented by Claire are effectively depicted. Caron is always the leader in their activities, and Inez, a colorless, sometimes whiny and dependent creature who seems a born follower, is her shadow. Claire regards them both with a mixture of amusement and irritation. She rarely expresses love for her prickly daughter, but her concern is revealed through her actions. Although ingenious murders are certainly not typical daily affairs for many contemporary single parents, the sometimes strained and distant relationships between nervous parents and adolescents who are testing their boundaries and attempting to find their own independent places in the world certainly are. Claire's wry, even sardonic, comments on her own feelings and actions add to her clearly recognizable portrayal.

An appeal to the experience of contemporary parents is clear in a number of episodes through all the novels. One small but telling example of such tensions occurs in *Strangled Prose* when, fearing that Caron is in possession of an important clue she and Inez may have stolen from a crime scene, Claire does something she knows Caron would fiercely resent: she invades her daughter's privacy:

At this point, I did something for which I shall always carry a gram or two of guilt. I searched Caron's room, from the dustiest corner under the bed to the crumb-infested top shelf in her closet. I was fairly sure she didn't have a silver medallion stashed somewhere, but I wanted to be certain. In the delivery room, mothers are given a few privileges in exchange for the unpleasantness; one is the inalienable right to pry. (*Strangled* 154)

What mother of a teenager could not respond with wry understanding to this passage!

In all the novels, Claire is central as narrator, detective, and protagonist. In all of them Caron, usually with Inez by her side—or a step or two behind—is also intimately involved, sometimes arousing Claire's maternal protective urges and always complicating life for herself and her mother. And in all of them, Peter Rosen is important, both as a detective and as Claire's friend and lover—but his importance in Claire's life is obviously less than is Caron's. Peter's importance, in fact, is perhaps on a level with that of the Book Depot, the bookstore which supports Claire financially and through which she finds professional fulfillment as well as a steady and reliable supply of reading material. Romantic and sexual life, while important, is subsidiary to the more pressing concerns of earning a living and fulfilling responsibilities to her daughter.

In other novels, not discussed here, Claire becomes involved in— and Hess makes perceptive, often pointed comments on—a variety of issues and trends in contemporary American life, some but not all of special interest to female readers. Such topics as the fad for mystery role-playing games (*The Murder at the Murder at the Mimosa Inn*), public education (*Dear Miss Demeanor*), the obsession of our culture with an unnatural slenderness (*A Diet to Die For*), and the theft of pets for use in scientific laboratories (*Roll Over and Play Dead*) indicate the breadth of Hess's concerns—and of Claire's involvements. In many ways, she is representative not only of American women but also of American middle-class society of her time, allowing her creator to satirize that society.

Also an appealing character, one who lives rather than proclaims her feminism, is Arly Hanks. The protagonist of Hess's second and, I would argue, somewhat less effective series, Arly is similar to Claire in some important ways and different in others; their differences result in significant variations in the appeals of and responses to the two characters and to their novels. Claire is portrayed as a fully rounded modern woman: bookseller, mother to Caron, and lover to Peter Rosen as well as amateur detective. Arly, in contrast, is less well rounded, being seen first and foremost as detective by virtue of her position as police chief, secondly as ironic commentator on the peculiar ways and people of Maggody, and only thirdly as daughter to Ruby Bee and woman with personal friendships and relationships. Like Claire, she is a woman doing work belonging more traditionally to men, but her job is far more conventionally masculine than Claire's.

Unlike Claire's, Arly's shattered marriage is not significant for having produced offspring. Its importance is simply that it explains her having lived away from Maggody for a number of years and thus having learned new and different attitudes toward her rustic home town and its odd denizens. As a former resident of Manhattan and member of its elite, she has seen a kind of life totally different from that to which she has now returned, and her resulting sophistication and knowledge of the world enable her to observe the rural Ozarks with ironic detachment (and when she revisits the city, in *Maggody in Manhattan,* she is able to describe it with an equal objectivity because of her grounding in the very different world of the Ozarks). In fact, her voice in the sections she narrates is not really very different from the objective auctorial voice of the omniscient third-person sections. All this suggests an appeal to a somewhat different, though overlapping, audience from that for which the Claire Malloy novels are apparently intended. The tone of her narratives may be illustrated by her first words to the reader (not, however, the opening words of her first novel):

Raz Buchanon stomped into the police department, his watery, red-rimmed eyes snapping and his whiskery chin several inches ahead of his nose. An aroma of sourness swept in on his heels. "Perkins stole my dawg, Arly! He plumb took it right out of my pen, and I want to know what in blazes you plan to do about it!"

I put down the block of wood I was whittling into a semblance of a duck. (*Malice in Maggody* 5-6)

In fact, to reverse a phrase which Adrienne Rich first used and then rejected, perhaps Arly speaks for the "ghostly [man] in all women" (69, 71). Her independent lifestyle and her profession as well as her clearly egalitarian and feminist attitudes do enable her to appeal to feminist readers. But the novel's greater concentration on satiric treatment of its locale and its heavy reliance on broad comedy, not to say farce, create a different tone. While the fact that Arly is a woman is of course important, her books could rather easily be rewritten to center on a male protagonist; such rewriting would be impossible for Claire Malloy's novels.

Another difference between the two series which also relates to their differing audience appeal is most easily defined by looking at their continuing characters. In Claire Malloy's series, the continuing characters in addition to Claire herself are primarily a group of her closest associates: Caron and Inez, of course, and Peter Rosen. In the Ozarks series, a much larger and more varied cast appears: there are of course Ruby Bee (Arly's mother), and Ruby Bee's close friend Estelle Oppers. There is also state trooper John Plover, introduced in *Malice in Maggody* and appearing occasionally in a role somewhat analogous though less important than Peter Rosen's in the Claire Malloy series.

In addition, and most strikingly, there is the clan of Buchanons, as varied in their kinks and perversions as any characters in William Faulkner or Erskine Caldwell. They are inbred and replete with mental retardation, ignorance, and venality, and some of the town's leading citizens, the more respectable appearing members of the clan including its mayor and the one police officer serving under Arly, come from their ranks. Some of them represent pure greed, others single-minded evil, and some just stupidity. Most are comic characters, and the reader's interest is diffused between them and Arly, the novel's nominal protagonist. Arly's narration reveals their similarities to Faulkner's Snopeses:

If all the Buchanons are confusing you, good luck. Half the residents of Stump County are Buchanons. Inbreeding and incest have produced the beetlish brow, beady amber eyes, and thick lips. Nothing in the way of intelligence has been produced. Buchanons are known for a certain amount of animal cunning, but nothing that would outwit an above-average raccoon. The other half of the Maggody PD and my loyal deputy, Paulie Buchanon, is smarter than most of his relatives; he's terribly sincere and determined to escape Maggody via the state police academy. Jim Bob's no dummy either, if holding the office of mayor for thirteen years is any indication. He pulled enough horse trades to put up the Kwik-Stoppe Shoppe (known to locals as the Kwik-Screw) and to build a brick house on a hilltop overlooking Boone Creek. He may have made an error when he married Barbara Ann Buchanon, his second cousin from over in Emmet. Everybody calls her Mrs. Jim Bob, a local and inexplicable tradition that's not worth dwelling on. (*Malice* 8)

Arly's function in these novels, in fact, seems in one light to be simply to give the reader a sympathetic character to take with some degree of seriousness, a single voice of sanity in a farcical world of lunatics of both the innocent and the depraved sorts.

As a writer, Hess is skilled and fluent; as a social critic, she can be incisive, even caustic; as a feminist, she imagines strong and independent women who manage to live fulfilling lives in a patriarchal society. Her primary contribution to the field of detective fiction, in addition to her creation of a gallery of interesting and amusing characters, may well be seen in her use of voice and tone to distinguish between the situations of her protagonists, both of them women who insist against odds on living lives which are both self-directed and productive, but who live these lives in contrasting familial, social, and geographical situations. Paradoxically, it is the woman who is less untraditional in her lifestyle—Claire Malloy—who is the more conscious of her daily struggles with that patriarchal world. The more unconventional woman—police chief Arly Hanks—seems to take her unusual work almost for granted (with amusement noting that she got the job because she was almost the only applicant, and certainly the only one with any qualifications). She concentrates more on the eccentricities and the problems surrounding her than on her personal life and situation.

Feminist readers must recognize in both these detectives figures to be admired, perhaps even emulated. In them, a contemporary woman writer is speaking, as Rich foresaw in 1971, as part of the creation of a new "balance," no longer "haunted by 'convention and propriety' [or] by internalized fears of being and saying themselves." This "woman who writes," in Spender's reminder of a significant definition of a feminist, uses her gift and her labor to illustrate possibilities. Not all of these possibilities are inspiring or particularly desirable, but they are very real in our world. Some women, like Arly, without stressing their feminism or even perhaps recognizing it, are successfully building or rebuilding their worlds around their work—and are doing that work well and finding fulfillment in it. Others, like Claire, are coping with the remains of lives once structured around traditional roles which, for various reasons, have become unplayable for them. In these characters, women readers must recognize themselves and laugh both at their own sometimes strained attempts to cope—and at their successes and failures. In these novels, unlike the traditional male canon Fetterley discussed so many years ago, women can find characters and situations which now allow them to "identify as [female] and be assured that to be female *is* "to be universal, to be American."

Works Cited

Fetterley, Judith. *The Resisting Reader: A Feminist Approach to American Fiction.* Bloomington: Indiana UP, 1978.

Hess, Joan. *Malice in Maggody.* New York: St. Martin's, 1987.

——. *Strangled Prose.* New York: St. Martin's, 1986.

Rich, Adrienne. *On Lies, Secrets, and Silence: Selected Prose 1966-1978.* New York: Norton, 1979.

Spender, Dale. *The Writing or the Sex? or Why You Don't Have to Read Women's Writing to Know It's No Good.* New York: Pergamon, 1989.

Gender and Voice in the Novels of Sarah Caudwell

Sharon A. Russell

Reading mysteries is always a guilty pleasure, an act of negotiation with the patriarchy. As Kathleen Klein states, "The predictable formula of detective fiction is based on a world whose sex/gender valuations reinforce male hegemony" (225). While Klein finds minimal changes in recent work in this conservative genre, she suggests several approaches to its reformulation: "A feminocentric novel does not necessarily need a feminist detective but it cannot evade questions of gender—intertwined with those of class, race, sexual preference, and social attitudes—if it is to succeed" (227). Her first suggestion is the substitution of crimes with social importance for the usual dead body. "[S]ocial injustice, industrial corruption, rape and battery are serious crimes which also ask the readers to rethink their expectations of fiction and life" (228). Klein would also replace female stereotypes with real women. But beyond such substitutions, Klein recommends a reconsideration of the basic structure of the genre. She favors abandoning closure with its reaffirmation of the status quo. The final quality of this re-vision of the genre involves a change in its articulation: "It is obvious that the male first-person narrator cannot truthfully tell a woman's story, but neither can an implicitly phallocentric third-person narrative voice which cleaves to the generic formula" (229). Klein proposes the replacement of the traditional narrator with multiple female voices. Yet another alternative is posited in the work of Sarah Caudwell: the ungendered first-person narrator. While a shift in voice is only one of the tactics Klein suggests, the imaginative stance taken by Caudwell deserves serious exploration as an attack on the patriarchal structure of the genre. Oxford Professor Hilary Tamar is the principal narrator of three mysteries by Caudwell: *Thus Was Adonis Murdered, The Shortest Way to Hades,* and *The Sirens Sang of Murder.* Tamar's gender is never indicated in these novels. This lack of gender identification either delights or infuriates the reader. "Very few people seemed to notice that there was any doubt. Usually they referred to Hilary as certainly female or certainly male. It's now mentioned in the jacket copy and, having been tipped off, readers become very angry at me for not resolving it at the end of the book" (Caudwell qtd. in Klaven 56). Caudwell also avers she will never reveal the gender of Tamar. "I think Hilary is sort of a quintessential Oxford don. . . . I don't really regard Oxford dons as being determined by gender" (56).

This last statement might suggest Caudwell's claim to innocence of any underlying feminist concerns in her writing. Her quotation might be rephrased by substituting the word "sex" for "gender." Oxford dons may not appear to be sexually determined; they would usually be linguistically gendered as male. Judith Butler suggests, "As a shifting and contextual phenomenon, gender does not denote a substantive being, but a relative point of convergence among culturally and historically specific sets of relations" (10). While Caudwell might not recognize the difference in these two terms (sex, gender) this lack on her part is an indication of a more general ignorance of the effects of her linguistic and literary decisions. Her selection of professions and her depiction of the other recurring characters in her novels clearly indicate an intent to enter into a dialogue with the mystery tradition. Her most recent work with its inclusion of parodies of romantic fiction and references to the mystery gives an even clearer indication of her self-conscious approach to the genre. A close examination of the three books reveals both her interest in exploring gender/sex relationships and the inherent dangers that accompany any attempt to alter the patriarchy from within.

All of the novels open with statements by Hilary Tamar concerning the nature of scholarship and truth. While this opening is formalized as a prologue in the two more recent works, *Thus Was Adonis Murdered* begins with a hyperbolic paean to Scholarship's pursuit of Ignorance without hope of reward or recognition. This language is immediately undercut by Tamar's humorous deflation of it. The Professor states the work is not even being undertaken for congratulations from those involved: "Which is very fortunate, because they don't" (7). In *The Shortest Way to Hades* the prologue parodies the usual first-person disclaimers about the veracity of the narrative: "Cost candour what it may, I will not deceive my readers. By some whim of the publishers, and despite my own protests, the ensuing narrative is to be offered to the public in the guise of a work of fiction" (7). *The Sirens Sang of Murder* continues Caudwell's tradition of apologizing for deferring yet again the appearance of Hilary Tamar's long-awaited treatise, *Causa in the Early Common Law,* with further excuses and justifications:

Scholarship, when applied to even such trifling questions, may dispel Error and reveal Truth that it will perhaps afford not only instruction to the public but much needed encouragement to other scholars. (1)

While linguistic parodies recur in a novel being written by two of the characters in *Sirens,* the mysteries themselves proceed through rather traditional first-person narration and a variety of forms of written communication from other characters.

The mysteries Professor Tamar solves are also strongly within British detective fiction traditions. In *Adonis* the murderer is merely greedy and the victim is not well known and therefore will not be missed. The impetus for the investigation is the accusation and detention of one of Hilary's friends. But even she is not placed in prison while Hilary investigates. Julia must only move to another, less grand hotel. The motive for the murder in *Hades* is linked to an inheritance. While the murderer tries to kill several people, she is only successful once. The victim is one of the least likable of the characters, and none of the really good people suffer. In *Sirens* sexual jealousy motivates the deaths. One occurs before the beginning of the novel, and the other victim is again one of the less admirable characters. The good are placed in danger, but they are rescued. In all cases order is restored, and those involved are inconvenienced but lose neither clients, friends, nor much money in the process.

While Caudwell makes no pretense of disrupting the genre on the level of plot, many of her literary devices also remain quite traditional. She varies Hilary's first person narrative with letters, telexes, and excerpts from guidebooks. Her characters exhibit the usual remarkable abilities to reproduce long conversations verbatim. At appropriate points in the narrative, Hilary expresses a knowledge of the solution before it is revealed to the reader allowing those who enjoy the puzzle time to formulate their own solutions. Such statements as, " 'As it happens,' I said, 'what is suspicious is that he didn't steal the holdall' " contain echoes of Sherlock Holmes (*Adonis* 167). Another response exploits the values of the Oxford education; Hilary's awareness of the dangers facing friends is based on a classical allusion: " 'I think,' I said, 'because Sebastian talked too much about Book XI of the Odyssey and the transmission of the texts of Euripides' " (*Hades* 172). In fact, if Hilary is to be believed, university training is essential for the detective: " 'I am a scholar,' I said. 'Few mysteries are impenetrable to the trained mind' " (*Hades* 177).

Caudwell's other characters have no trouble understanding Hilary because most of them share her educational background. One of the continuing characters, Timothy Shepherd, is her former student. Only Michael Cantrip is singled out as a Cambridge graduate; the rest of the cast are all products of Oxford. Most of them even inhabit the same law offices, and Julia Larwood, the tax expert, has offices next door. They are all good friends, exhibiting little professional jealousy, and Julia and Michael were even romantically involved at one point. Selena Jardine and Desmond Ragwort are about the same age as Julia, while Timothy, who is notable for his absence from much of the action after the first novel, is older and their senior in the firm. Hilary stays at his flat for short periods of time, but for longer visits the professor finds other accommodations. However, once Caudwell dispenses with their basic characterization, these friends and associates do not remain stereotypes. Not only does Caudwell give each a unique personality and style but also as a group they are unconventional.

All of these young people are successful members of the English Bar, and gender seems to have no impact on their pursuit of their profession. Even though Julia is often depicted as a parody of the absent-minded professional, all acknowledge her skill with complex tax laws. They do, of course, display a variety of physical characteristics, but they are all young and attractive. Aside from her foregrounding their equality, Caudwell's most important means of distinguishing them, and her writing, is to deal directly with their sexuality. Such direct references to sexual activity are not usual in this type of British mystery. And while their encounters are not presented graphically, her characters participate in the kind of brief sensual encounters most often detailed in the American hard-boiled tradition. These lawyers are, for the most part, interested in sex only as a diversion rather than as the basis of an ongoing relationship. Caudwell's depiction of these characters' attitudes towards sex are the first indications of her challenge of the traditional British mystery. But her treatment of this subject also raises questions about her vision of the woman's position in society.

Adonis opens with Julia's trip to Venice with a group of art lovers. Her friends waste no time letting it be understood by the reader and, incidentally, Hilary (who must already know) exactly what she was looking for on the trip.

"Julia has been working very hard all summer," said Selena . . . . "My only fear is that she may be over-precipitate. I have reminded her that young men like to think one is interested in them as people: if one discloses too early the true nature of one's interest, they are apt to be offended and get all hoity-toity." (17)

This passage demonstrates more than just a frank discussion of sexual desire: in Caudwell's universe women are usually the sexual aggressors. Julia's involvement in the murder comes from her pursuing her interest in a young man, one of the art lovers. Julia who has also has a brief fling with a waiter is detained because she claims to have been in bed with Ned at the time medical evidence indicates he was murdered. In *Sirens* two women engineer a reversal which allows the married one a night with Cantrip. However in this novel, marital infidelity is the motive for murder. While the husband exhibits the jealousy, and he, for the most part, attacks other men rather than his wife, the use of this kind of motive validates this emotion as a position worth killing for. Women's control of sexual desire leads to other areas of dominance in relationships. When Selena and Sebastian go sailing on their vacation in Hades, Selena is the captain of the ship.

Caudwell does not deal exclusively with heterosexual relationships. Ned, the Adonis of the book with that title, is one half of a homosexual couple. In a complex series of events, Kenneth (Ned's lover) kills so Ned can assume the identity and lifestyle of the dead man. Kenneth explains: "I knew I had to do it for you. I saw it was the only way of you having the kind of life you ought to have and I knew I ought to give it to you" (238). Ned exhibits an ambiguous sexuality when Julia seduces him. Although it is hard to see how she could have missed the relationship between two young men traveling together, she writes endlessly of her attraction to Ned, the handsome one in the partnership. She remains oblivious to homosexual possibilities even when Ned tells her not to tell Kenneth about their sexual encounter (113). None of those reading her letter get a hint of a possible relationship between Ken and Ned either. The only character who suggests anything about Ned's sexual preferences is the Major, who is constantly pursuing Julia and therefore thought to have a vested interest in discrediting the competition. The group finally learns from another lawyer of Ken's grand passion for Ned.

While homosexuality is treated like any other love relationship when it is finally acknowledged, the possibility of a lesbian attraction is treated more problematically in two of the three novels. In both cases Julia, who otherwise is depicted as the pursuer of eligible males, is involved. Just after she has been accused of killing Ned, various members of the group forward hypotheses to suggest how Julia might have been involved with the dead man. Ragwort proposes a scenario where Marylou, a young American traveling with an often absent businessman husband, misunderstands Julia's friendship. Julia has already written a letter describing the events leading to Marylou's husband's discovering them together. As he enters the room, Julia, wearing few clothes because Marylou is mending her slip, is comforting Marylou who has been crying over the lack of love in her marriage. Ragwort suggests Marylou became jealous and killed Ned: "There had been, in short, nothing in Julia's manner to indicate that she would recoil from an advance with loathing and abhorrence. If, indeed, that is what she would have done" (84). Selena rather quickly defends her friend against this suggestion. "If you mean . . . that Julia is not the sort of woman who would wantonly wound anyone's feelings, particularly those of a girl who had been kind to her and was alone and friendless in a strange country—" (84). Since this scenario is never advanced again, it functions only as a means of creating ambiguity. In *Adonis* Caudwell's various presentations of female sexuality become part of her strategy for reinforcing the neutral gender of the narrator. In a world filled with role reversals and sexual ambiguity Hilary's lack of gender can be more easily disguised.

The references to Julia and lesbianism in *Sirens* move from problematic to offensive. As this novel opens, Cantrip relates how he has learned of Julia's actions. She has, in the past, given a man Cantrip meets the impression she is a lesbian. Cantrip is shocked when this man tells him she was "like one of those ancient Greek birds who fancied other birds instead of chaps" (19). Cantrip defends her as "one of the keenest chap fanciers I knew" (19). After reading this telex Julia explains her actions to the rest of the group. She had chosen lesbianism as an excuse because she didn't want to damage her chance of future business relationships with this man when she rejected him.

"On the other hand, Stingham and Grynne use his firm for most of their work in Jersey, and quite often instruct me in connection with the same matters, so I was reluctant to express myself with the degree of rudeness which would evidently be required to persuade him of his error. I thought the tactful thing would be to give the impression that my repugnance was general rather than particular." (21)

Selena finds this approach sensible and is sorry Cantrip spoils Julia's excuse. What is a profound life choice for women becomes no more than a means of protecting a possible business connection. Caudwell's light treatment of such a serious subject raises questions about the way she chooses to portray women. Her model for female liberation seems to involve nothing more than the concept of sexual role reversal. And even this approach is treated with an inappropriate tone even for a comic novel of manners. It should be obvious to any author, especially one dealing directly with female sexuality, that serious life decisions are not an appropriate source of humor in a patriarchal world. Another example of Caudwell's problematic treatment of female characters occurs in Timothy's description of his first encounter with Julia after the murder in *Adonis*. Up to this point Timothy, unlike Cantrip, has been presented as an objective narrator. His usual verbal style is clever, but he does not use classical metaphors in other passages in this letter:

"Physically, at any rate, her recent difficulties seemed to have done Julia no harm. There has been, it is true, some increase in her customary dishevelment: she looks like one of Priam's daughters after a more than usually trying rape— but one, all the same, who during the Siege of Troy has eaten well, slept well and done plenty of sunbathing." (147)

Even if such a statement could be considered an element of characterization, an author concerned with the position of women in society could easily have another character challenge it. Such negative examples must throw doubt on Caudwell's entire project.

Some might find Caudwell's refusal to gender her narrator as a triumphant examination of sex roles in society. In *Voice* Andrew Klavan praises her: "Hilary's androgyny is the central statement of a keenly self-aware and parodic intelligence intent on examining the constraints of sex roles, the mechanics of ravishment and the thrills and dangers of seduction and disguise" (55). The dust jackets of her books are full of praise for Caudwell's style and wit. Even Amanda Cross is cited on the back of one book. But critics like Klavan do not recognize that gender does not disappear in the character of Hilary Tamar. On one level class becomes the substitute for sex in Caudwell's creation of Hilary's identity, making it the site of difference. While sexual role reversals undermine gender differences, the homogeneous class values represented by the characters' university educations and status in society reaffirm these values.

Caudwell's characters are, after all, lawyers. The law they support is the law of the patriarchy. When class is substituted for gender there is even less of a challenge to this law. As Trinh T. Minh-ha states,

A social regulator and a political potential for change, gender, in its own way, baffles definition. It escapes the "diagnostic power" of a sex-oriented language/sex-identified logic and coincides thereby with difference, whose inseparable temporal and spatial dynamics produces the illusion of identity while undermining it relentlessly. (116)

The sexual role reversals and ambiguities of Caudwell's novels are literary devices which help create a world where Hilary's non-gendered status can be easily maintained. While Caudwell makes no claims for a feminist stance, her use of sex and gender have caused many to view her writing as a "breakthrough" for the mystery genre. Hilary's first-person, ungendered voice succeeds as a literary device because this character is not seen by the other characters, not presented visually to the reader. The erasure of the body in Caudwell's work is equal to an erasure of sex. In a world where all of the characters are concerned about sexual identity and sexual activity, the absence of sex gives rise to the lack of gender. The texts do not erase the culturally determined polarities inherent in their presentation of gender because the concept of sexual oppositions is reinforced through the emphasis on such distinctions within the work. Even those exchanges of identity between characters which form a recurring theme in Caudwell's texts support sexual polarities such as female/female or male/male exchanges which also maintain heterosexual/homosexual oppositions. In the final chapter of her analysis of gender Butler states:

Indeed, when the subject is said to be constituted, that means simply that the subject is a consequence of certain rule-governed discourses that govern the intelligible invocation of identity. The subject is not determined by the rules through which it is generated because signification is not a founding act, but rather a regulated process of repetition that both conceals itself and enforces its rules precisely through the production of substantializing effects. (145)

She also suggests that the very process of repetitive signifying will produce failures which will provide the tools to challenge the distinctions of gender. She finds one such subversion in parody which can constitute the real as an effect: "As the effects of a subtle and politically enforced performativity, gender is an 'act,' as it were, that is open to splittings, self-parody, self-criticism, and those hyperbolic exhibitions of 'the natural' that, in their very exaggeration, reveal its fundamentally phantasmatic status" (146-47). But Caudwell's use of comedy and parody remain within the tradition of class and sex which reinforce rather than challenge the rules for constituting the subject's gender.

Up to this point I have used the voice of the scholar, but I must now speak in whatever voice I have managed to retrieve from the patriarchy. As Trinh T. Minh-ha states, "Stolen language will always remain that other's language" (20). I began this study interested in the feminist implications of a non-gendered voice. As I looked more closely at Caudwell's novels I tried to withhold judgment. I was not going to condemn her if she did not successfully counter the patriarchal elements of the genre. I was even willing to settle for works that omitted some of the criteria suggested by Klein. Klein would like mysteries without bodies, mysteries dealing with other crimes connected to women. O.K. so there are bodies. Klein explores the possibilities of open texts, texts that do not reproduce the closure demanded by the patriarchy. O.K. Hilary solves the crime. But the more I read the less I like the tone of Caudwell's work. Isn't mere role reversal a way of playing the patriarchy's games? Is the refusal to identify a character's sex an act of defiance or a means of ignoring the possible effects of such an absence. As Maria Black and Rosalind Coward state:

We see one of the major political problems confronting feminism to be the need to force men to recognize themselves as men. The discursive formation which allows men to represent themselves as non-gendered and to define women constantly according to their sexual status is a discursive formation with very definite effects. It allows men to deny the effect of their gendered subjectivity on women. (132)

The denial of gender remains only a literary device because it is not a valid option. "I" cannot equal "it," especially in a society where the absence of a specific reference usually leads to the identification of the subject as the universal male. Is Hilary a man because he isn't given a gender, or is Hilary a female because the need to protect her identity makes her seem passive?

I begin to question my own sense of humor when I reread these mysteries, but I cannot find any reference to rape humorous. I cannot find a woman who deals with lesbianism as plot device worth discussing in a feminist context. Am I just being petty? Are liberals more dangerous than conservatives?

I am used to arriving at my own form of closure when writing a paper. I like to find the universals, arrive at the truths, conflicting though they might be and state them in a final paragraph. Are conflicting yet universal truths another negotiation with the patriarchy? What is it about this study that allows me conclusions but no closure? Is it a sense of betrayal? Has Caudwell betrayed the hope and promise I felt when I originally started this study? I now wonder how any woman could write some of the things she has written. All work is a voyage of discovery. In this work I have discovered I cannot make those general, impersonal statements that would bring closure. How have questions about gender brought me to this position? Is it anger that has placed me beyond conclusions generated by language? Any woman has the right to speak. But I, as a woman, also have the right to object to what she says and how she says it. And only by continuing to question can I ever hope reach a place where such objections are no longer necessary.

Works Cited

Black, Maria, and Rosalind Coward. "Linguistic, social and sexual relations: a review of Dale Spender's Man Made Language." *The Feminist Critique of Language: A Reader*. Ed. Deborah Cameron. New York: Routledge, 1990. 111-33.

Butler, Judith. *Gender Trouble: Feminism and the Subversion of Identity*. New York: Routledge, 1990.

Caudwell, Sarah. *The Shortest Way to Hades*. New York: Viking-Penguin,1986.

——.*The Sirens Sang of Murder*. New York: Delacorte, 1989.

——. *Thus Was Adonis Murdered*. New York: Viking-Penguin, 1982.

Klavan, Andrew. "Playing With a Different Sex: Sarah Caudwell's Role Call." *Voice* 9 Jan. 1990.

Klein, Kathleen Gregory. *The Woman Detective: Gender and Genre*. Urbana: U of Illinois P, 1988.

Minh-ha, Trinh T. *Woman, Native, Other*. Bloomington: Indiana UP, 1989.

The Re-Imagining of Cordelia Gray

Joan G. Kotker

One of my favorite fictional characters is P.D. James's detective, Cordelia Gray, as she appears in *An Unsuitable Job for a Woman*. In this character James has drawn an excellent portrait of the outsider, showing the skills the outsider must develop in order to survive in a world where she does not fit, the longing to be a part of that world that she must in some way resolve, and the value system she develops that allows her to have self-regard in a world that has little regard for her. As someone who grew up working class, Hispanic, Catholic and female in an affluent Anglo-Saxon community, I found James's description of Gray to be both moving and convincing. However, James's second Cordelia Gray novel, *The Skull Beneath the Skin,* presents a revisionist portrait that undermines Gray's initial worldview and in doing so, weakens her as a heroic figure. It is as though James, alarmed at having created a strong, atypical female hero, felt compelled to go back and recast her in a more traditional mold.

In her first appearance in *Unsuitable Job* Gray is hired by Sir Ronald Callender to investigate the suicide of his son, Mark, until recently a student at Cambridge. Sir Ronald ostensibly wants to know why Mark killed himself, but in fact Mark was murdered by Sir Ronald, who has hired Gray because he knows that someone was at the scene of the crime either during or just after Mark's death; he is afraid that whoever it was may have knowledge of his own role in the killing. Sir Ronald is confident that whatever Gray's findings are, he can control her and her information so that he will learn what he wants to know without endangering himself, but this does not turn out to be the case: although Gray succeeds in discovering who was at the scene of the crime, she also discovers that it was Sir Ronald who committed the murder. He has killed Mark because he needs Mark's inheritance to support his scientific laboratories. Sir Ronald believes that the work of the labs will bring far more good to the world than the life of one person could possibly do, and so the sacrifice of Mark is justified. Eliza Leaming, Sir Ronald's long-time mistress and business manager, overhears Cordelia explaining to him how she knows that he is the murderer of Mark and Leaming kills Sir Ronald in an act of vengeance: Leaming is Mark's unacknowledged mother. Gray then conspires with Leaming to present Sir Ronald's death as a suicide, just as he has presented his son's. Ultimately Gray succeeds, doing so in the face of a Scotland Yard power structure that is determined to break her.

Throughout the novel, we are given a great deal of background information on Gray. She initially becomes an outsider through two events, one beyond anyone's control and the other, clearly controllable. In the first instance, her mother dies shortly after her birth and in the second, her father's response is to isolate the baby Cordelia even more: where nature has taken away her mother, he takes himself away as father, leaving her to be placed in a series of foster homes. Here, Gray develops a crucial skill of the outsider, the ability to accurately assess the world around her and on the basis of that assessment, acquire the protective coloring that will enable her to survive in a place where she does not fit. James says, "Cordelia had early learnt stoicism. All her foster parents, kindly and well-meaning in their different ways, had demanded one thing of her—that she should be happy. She had quickly learned that to show unhappiness was to risk the loss of love" (22). This seems a terrible thing for a child to have to learn—surely happiness ought to be a natural condition of childhood and not an assumed emotion. James goes on to say of Gray wearing a mask of happiness, "Compared with this early discipline of concealment, all subsequent deceits had been easy" (22). This is both a pronouncement of what has been in Gray's life and of what is to come: we are led to understand that there have been many subsequent deceits, and we are also prepared for the final, successful deceit which will be the climax of the novel.

When Gray leaves the world of foster homes, it is to enter a world where she is again an outsider, that of a Roman Catholic convent school. She is here through a combination of her own actions and blind luck. She has done very well on her eleven-plus scholarship exams and her records have been confused with those of another "C. Gray," who is a Roman Catholic. When the school discovers its mistake, Gray is already a student there. Since her father, an itinerant Marxist poet intent on saving the world rather than caring for his daughter, does not reply to the nun's letters explaining what has happened, they keep her on at the convent for what turn out to be "the six most settled and happy years of her life," years in which "for the first time she learned that she needn't conceal her intelligence, that cleverness which a succession of foster mothers had somehow seen as a threat" (86). The convent itself serves the function of doubling the outsider image, since just as the "incorrigibly Protestant" Gray is an outsider among the Catholic nuns, so too are they outsiders in Protestant England. Although Gray is sheltered and nurtured by the community of nuns, it is a community that is ultimately unable to give Gray access to the world of the insider as it is defined in this novel. For Gray, such access would be attained through Cambridge University, a place that she sees in heartbreakingly pastoral terms. Here she would be in the world of the mind, a world open to her because of the meritocracy of intellectual achievement, but in his greatest act of abandonment, her father denies her this world. Instead of allowing her to go for a scholarship to Cambridge, when she turns sixteen he takes her out of the convent and she begins "her wandering life as cook, nurse, messenger and general camp follower to Daddy and the comrades" (87). James illustrates here the powerlessness of outsiders: the nuns, who can prepare Gray for Cambridge, cannot override her father's decision to bar her access to the university. As with Mark Callender, Gray is sacrificed by her father to his fantasy of the good of the whole.

The pattern of children being denied the life of the mind in order to serve fathers and surrogate fathers is similarly illustrated in the fate of Sir Ronald Callendar's lab assistant, Chris Lunn. Just as Gray has been taken out of school to serve her father, Lunn is taken out of a juvenile detention home to serve Sir Ronald in his microbiology lab. Obviously a lab is a better place to be than a detention home, but in removing Lunn from the home, Sir Ronald has acted for his own benefit rather than for Lunn's; when Lunn turns out to be gifted at science, Sir Ronald refuses to educate him, explaining to Cordelia that to have done so would have been to lose a fine lab technician. In these two examples, caretakers serve their own interests rather than the interests of those in their care. In the world of P.D. James, it is very costly to be a child or a subordinate.

In his final act of abandonment Grey's father dies and she returns to England to begin to make a life for herself but with little means to do so other than the secretarial skills she has, fittingly, taught herself. Bernie Pryde of Pryde's Detective Agency hires her as a temporary typist and after a few weeks, begins to train her as a detective. We can surmise that like Lunn she shows aptitude for this new work, but unlike Sir Ronald Callender, Bernie offers to make her a partner. However, Bernie is himself an outsider: he has been forced out of Scotland Yard's CID for what we infer was graft and he can now never be the official detective he once wanted to be. Pryde's Detective Agency is his poor substitute for Scotland Yard and it can exist only outside the orthodoxy, just as the Roman Catholic nuns who were Gray's earlier teachers exist outside the orthodoxy of Protestant England.

While both Pryde and Gray acknowledge their outsider roles, they do so in the midst of great nostalgia for what might have been. Pryde trains Gray just as he was trained in the CID in such skills as "how to search the scene of a crime properly, how to collect exhibits, some elementary self-defence, how to detect and lift fingerprints," and it is that official Scotland Yard world that forms his reference points for whatever the issue at hand (32). He quotes Adam Dalgliesh, his superintendent at the Yard, over and over in his instruction of Gray: "Never theorize in advance of your facts" (42). When examining the site of the crime, "ask yourself what you saw, not what you expected to see or what you hoped to see, but what you saw" (70). Most significant, Dalgliesh as quoted by Bernie is the source of the wisdom that allows Cordelia to solve the case: "Get to know the dead person. Nothing about him is too trivial, too unimportant. Dead men can talk. They can lead you directly to their murderer" (43). Ironically, when Dalgliesh interrogates Cordelia after the death of Sir Ronald, attempting to break her story, it is Bernie's professional knowledge, perhaps derived once again from Dalgliesh, that sustains her: "In this country, if people won't talk, there's nothing you can do to make them" (274). At the end of the novel Gray charges Dalgliesh with being yet another caretaker who has abandoned his task, saying, "You sacked [Bernie]. All he ever wanted was to be a detective and you wouldn't give him a chance" (284). Worse is her accusation, "And after you'd sacked him, you never enquired how he got on. You didn't even come to [his] funeral!" (283). Showing one of the qualities that have endeared him as a series detective to James's readers, the self-reflective Dalgliesh later says to his superior, "Cordelia Gray was right. I ought to have enquired what happened to Bernie Pryde," and when the superior tells him that it was not part of his duty, Dalgliesh says, "Of course not. But then one's more serious neglects seldom are part of one's duty," again emphasizing the underlying theme of neglect on the part of those in positions of responsibility (286). At the end of the novel readers agree with Dalgliesh that Bernie has had his revenge because like Dalgliesh we know that "whatever mischief that child [Gray] was up to in Cambridge, she was working under [Bernie's] direction" (286).

Just as Gray in her accusation of Dalgliesh arrives at resolution of a kind for Bernie and his longing to be a Scotland Yard detective, so too does she arrive at resolution of her longing for Cambridge and the life of the university. When she goes there to learn more about Mark, she immediately feels at home, in her rightful place. She thinks that "in her wanderings she had seen lovelier places, but none in which she had been happier or more at peace. How indeed . . . could the heart be indifferent to such a city where stone and stained glass, water and green lawns, trees and flowers were arranged in such ordered beauty for the service of of learning" (87-88). Gray goes on the Cam in a punt with friends of Mark. They seem to offer her the opportunity of being an insider at Cambridge, and "Cordelia knew how close she had come to giving up the case. She had been suborned by the beauty of the day, by sunshine, indolence, the promise of comradeship, even friendship, into forgetting why she was here" (122). In these Cambridge scenes James makes compelling the outsider's deep wish to belong and at the same time, she shows again the need for the outsider to be an acute observer of the world around her. As it turns out, Gray is correct in her reading of the situation: Mark's friends are indeed trying to charm her into abandoning the case, and she will never be one of them. Whatever promise Cambridge once offered her has been denied her, and she cannot bring it back with boat rides. Because she recognizes this she is able go on to solve the case.

Given her rejection of the friendship offered—even if spuriously— by Mark's friends, it is ironic that the loner Gray forms a close bond with the dead Mark, a bond that allows her to ultimately discover his killer. She finds many similarities between Mark and herself. They have each lost their mothers when very young, each has been raised by strangers (Mark was sent to boarding school at the age of five), each is a loner, each has a father who has dedicated his life to abstract notions of the good of all and each, we are led to believe, was unloved. They are the same age and Mark has been a part of Gray's fantasied Eden, Cambridge University. Gray emphasizes the closeness she feels to Mark by wearing his sweaters and his belt, a belt that, along with Bernie Pryde's gun, becomes her talisman and is instrumental in saving her life. Ultimately, she is Mark's avenger, protecting his father's murderer not for the sake of the murderer but for the sake of Mark, who deserved better of life than a father who killed him in the service of an idea. When Gray does this, she is avenging herself, too, putting herself on the line (she could, after all, be jailed for her complicity in covering up Sir Ronald's murder) to make the statement that children should be loved and the caretakers responsible for them held accountable. When, at the end of the novel, Dalgliesh and the Assistant Commissioner are discussing the crime and the fact that Leaming in all probability killed Sir Ronald, the Commissioner asks Dalgliesh if he thinks that Gray has deluded herself and actually believes that Sir Ronald committed suicide. Attesting to Gray's clear-sightedness Dalgliesh answers, "I don't think that young woman deludes herself about anything." He adds that he is glad the investigation is closed: "I dislike being made to feel during a perfectly ordinary interrogation that I'm corrupting the young" (286). The use of the word "corrupting" is an interesting one, and in fact, it is what Dalgliesh is attempting to do: Gray has given her word to Leaming that she will report Sir Ronald's death as suicide. In attempting to make her break her word, Dalgliesh is asking her to accept the value system of the world of insiders, to act, as her father and Mark's father have done, in terms of an abstract good, an abstract justice. That she will not do so marks her as an outsider who has developed her own, individual value system and who has the courage to hold to it.

In sum, then, in the character of Cordelia Gray as she appears in *An Unsuitable Job for a Woman,* P.D. James has created a very brave young woman who has the courage to call to task the overseers of the world. As an outsider and loner, she has much in common with such traditional fictional heroes as Huck Finn, Nick Adams, Hawkeye, and Shane. Like them, she rejects the values of her society, developing instead her own code. Her message is that although we cannot control the events of the world around us, we can control how we react to those events and can choose the individual stance we take before the world.

This was a powerful message for women coming of age in the early 1970s, who saw in Gray and her defeat of the patriarchy, a hero for women. Readers looked forward to subsequent Cordelia Gray novels, novels that would reflect what it is to be a woman in the contemporary world, but James's only other Cordelia Gray novel, *The Skull Beneath the Skin,* is very disappointing. Published ten years after *Unsuitable Job, Skull'*s plot is reminiscent of a Golden Age puzzle novel. Actress Clarissa Lisle has been receiving a series of what appear to be death threats. These are sent to her on the opening day of a new play's run and then at intervals throughout the duration of the play. Gray is hired by Lisle's husband to accompany her to Courcy Island, where she is to appear in an amateur production of *The Duchess of Malfi.* Gray's task is to intercept any threats and, if possible, find out who is making them. Despite Gray's presence, Lisle is killed, but the resolution to the puzzle is murky, lacking the neatness and emotional satisfaction of *Unsuitable Job'*s ending. Lisle has been killed by her stepson, Simon, who struck out at her in revulsion after she attempted to seduce him. Ambrose Gorringe, owner of the island, was being blackmailed by Lisle and conspires with Simon to hide his part in the death. Gorringe in turn attempts to kill the stepson by first of all not interfering in his suicide attempt and then by slamming down the trap door to a shaft that is rapidly filling with water, creating the possibility that the boy will drown. Thus the first murder is actually manslaughter, and one could argue that the second one is, too. Gorringe is not brought to justice, and we are led to believe that he will relish the fight to remain free. At the end of the novel his chances of doing so seem excellent: he has convincing explanations for everything that has happened, explanations that will surely seem more credible to the police and the courts than Gray's claim that this respected, well-to-do man is involved in murder. Thus, when the novel ends Gray is a failure, having been unable to either protect Lisle or prove that Gorringe is responsible for Simon's death.

This image of Gray as a failure is certainly not what one might have expected from her introduction in *Unsuitable Job*. In fact, the outcome of the second book makes one wonder if P.D. James has not had second thoughts, has perhaps come to agree with those characters in the first novel who tell Gray that detecting is an unsuitable job for a woman. Many of the events in the second novel echo those of the first, but in each case, they are treated in such a way as to cast doubt on the credibility of the initial event and of Gray's interpretation of it. A striking example is the portrait of Gray's father that we are given in the two works. Readers familiar with Gray's description of him in *Unsuitable Job* as the archetype of the caretaker who abandons his role, the parent who sacrifices his child's needs to his own, will be astonished to discover that she now feels he was someone "I think I could have liked . . . if we'd had time" (96). The reader wonders what sort of time Gray has in mind here: time to rewrite their history as parent and child? And why this change in perception anyway? It is introduced very awkwardly, as though James knows that she has a problem with credibility here, in a two-page discussion that opens with a character saying to Cordelia, with reference to absolutely nothing, "This may be a stupid question. Gray isn't an uncommon name. But you're not by any chance related to Redvers Gray?" When Gray answers that he was her father, the questioner explains his question by saying, "There's something about [your] eyes." He goes on to tell her that he had met her father "only once, but his was a face one didn't forget." Since the meeting would have been some forty years previously, the reader can be forgiven for being skeptical of this scene—surely there are more convincing ways to introduce the topic of Redvers Gray. In the ensuing conversation between Gray and her questioner, Ivo Whittingham, we learn that Redvers Gray had a great influence on his generation at Cambridge, that "he had the gift of making rhetoric sound sincere." Whittingham adds, "I should like to have known him." James has Gray respond, "So should I," but instead of her answer being an indictment of her father, it is the occasion for our being asked to reconsider our earlier harsh judgment of him. Whittingham says, "It was like that, was it? The revolutionary idealist dedicated to mankind in the abstract but not much good at caring for his own child." The "not much good" is certainly an understatement for describing a father who showed no interest at all in the fate of his child, but Whittingham then adds, "Not that I can criticize. I haven't done too well with mine." The suggestion here seems to be that fathers are like that and perhaps no more should be expected of them. When Gray then reflects back on the short time she spent with her father as all-purpose secretarial staff and domestic, she thinks, "that period of her life was passed, finished. And she hoped that they had given something to each other, if only trust" (95-96). Readers familiar with the first novel can be forgiven for wondering exactly what there might have been for Gray to trust in—the likelihood that her father would continue to exploit her? And is he in turn supposed to have trusted that she would allow him to do so?

The redrawing of Redvers Gray is completed when we learn that his daughter has benefited from her association with him after all. It seems that he left her a small inheritance (most improbably explained) that has allowed her to purchase a loft apartment in London. In sum, then, we are asked to rethink Gray's earlier portrait of her father, and since there is no plot necessity for this revision, it is puzzling to know why James has included it, especially as it throws doubt on Gray's earlier perceptions. When this train of thought is pursued, it undermines even the denouement of *Unsuitable Job*. Gray has seen herself in that novel as being much like its victim Mark Callender, partly because of the way they have been treated by their respective fathers. But if Gray was wrong about her own father, perhaps she is wrong about Mark's, in which case she has committed a grave injustice in helping to hide the fact that he was murdered. Since her stature as a character is based on the strength and courage that enable her to help his murderer because it is morally right in the context of the novel to do so, the suggestion that Gray may have misread the context seriously undermines her heroic role.

There are a number of other scenes in *Skull* that are reworkings of scenes in *Unsuitable Job*. For example, each novel has a description of a now-elderly woman who, when younger, suffered the death of an illegitimate child. In *Unsuitable Job* this woman is a key element in the plot, since her returning compulsively to the well where her child drowned all those years ago enables her to see that something is different, the cover has been moved. When she goes to examine it, she finds and rescues Gray, and not so incidentally begins to come to terms with her own guilt and loss. In *Skull*, there is a similar scene in which Whittingham tells Gray about the death of Miss Tolgarth's illegitimate daughter. Tolgarth is Lisle's dresser. One night at the theatre, Lisle received a phone call saying that Tolgarth's four-year-old daughter, who was in the hospital, had had a relapse and that Tolgarth should go at once. Lisle changed the message, telling Tolgarth that the hospital wanted her to go after the performance, that there was no urgency. The result was that when Tolgarth arrived at the hospital, her daughter was dead. Gray responds to this story by saying, "I don't understand how Miss Tolgarth can go on working for [Lisle]. I couldn't," and when Whittingham very reasonably points out that Gray is working for Lisle at that very moment, she says, "But that's different; at least I shall persuade myself that it is" (103). This feels like moral equivocation on the part of Gray, who in *Unsuitable Job* took it as her duty to challenge and unmask the negligent caretakers of the world, a role that clearly fits Tolgarth's employer, Lisle, in this instance. While there is some plot justification for the Tolgarth scene, it does not depend on Gray's response, a response that once more has the effect of reducing Gray as a heroic figure.

Yet another echo of *Unsuitable Job* in *Skull* is found in the well scene. As noted above, in the first novel Gray is thrown into a deep, narrow well, and it is a testament to her courage and willpower that she is able to work herself up to the top of the well so that when Miss Markland examines it, she is able to save Gray. This is a fine example of women working together to save a woman, and it is one of the emotional high points of the novel. In *Skull* there is a similar well-like shaft in a cave that is filled by the ocean at high tide. The shaft is covered by a trap door, and the minute the reader is introduced to it, she thinks, "Oh, no! Don't go near the shaft, Cordelia. It's going to be the well all over again!" Lo and behold, in what is almost a parody of *Unsuitable Job*'s well scene, Lisle's stepson, Simon, handcuffs himself to the ladder on the inside of the shaft and tosses away the key, planning to commit suicide by drowning as the water slowly rises. One might well ask why Simon has chosen this harrowing, long-drawn-out method, since we have already been given a scene in which he thinks about swimming out to sea and drowning, casting his vision of such a death in a peaceful, halcyon light. Whatever Simon's reasons, Gray finds him, talks him out of the suicide attempt, goes in the shaft to retrieve the key, unlocks the handcuffs, and then the trap door is slammed shut and locked on the two of them. Their only hope is to swim underwater to where the cave has its outlet into the sea. Gray succeeds in doing so but Simon does not. Thus, in this well scene, the young person strapped to the side is not rescued, as Gray was, and Gray can save only herself, suggesting that she is less powerful than the elderly Miss Markland, who succeeded in *Unsuitable Job*'s rescue attempt.

A final key element in *Skull* that again has the effect of undermining Gray's stature is that of the description of the detective agency itself. In *Unsuitable Job* the detective agency is a bare, dour place worthy of Philip Marlowe. "The staircase smelt . . . of stale sweat, furniture polish and disinfectant. The walls were dark green and were invariably damp whatever the season as if they secreted a miasma of desperate respectability and defeat." Inside the office is an "oblong of garish rug which Bernie had recently bought in the hope of impressing visitors . . . but which Cordelia privately thought had only drawn attention to the shabbiness of the rest of the office" (11). There is one other employee besides Gray, a temporary typist named Miss Sparshott whose face is "blotched with resentment, her back as rigid as the space bar," and who, we are led to believe, will leave after Bernie's death since she has neither ties to nor liking for Gray (10). This is in sharp contrast to the office described in *Skull*. Although it is the same office, the stairway has improved to the point where its identifying characteristics are only that it is narrow and steep, the smell having disappeared between books, and the office that was once so bleak now has its walls painted a soft yellow, plants on every surface, and even a cat's basket in the outer room. This redecorated agency is still shabby, but now it is the shabbiness of comfortable domesticity rather than that of a small business run on the desperate edge of bankruptcy. In this office Gray again has temporary employees, Beavis and Miss Maudsley, but they are a far cry from Miss Sparshott. Beavis is a dancer working as a typist while he rests, and Miss Maudsley is a "gentle, sixty-two-year-old rector's sister, eking out her pension in a bedsitting-room in South Kensington," and neither feels all that temporary: the suggestion is that their work at Pryde's is the only work they have (4). Beavis and Maudsley get on with one another very well, so that "life in the outer office became very cosy at times" (5). Unlike Miss Sparshott, the two employees are very fond of Cordelia, as she is of them. There is no plot reason for their being here; all they do is add a sort of domestic feel to Pryde's Detective Agency and change Gray's image from that of a loner to that of a member of an extended family.

If this cozy office with its plants and cheerful chatter seems a far cry from the classic office of the P.I. described in *Unsuitable Job,* it is exactly right for the clients who come to Pryde's Detective Agency in *Skull,* since Gray's agency has changed from the all-purpose one with its aura of the hard-boiled described in the first novel to one that specializes in finding lost pets. In *Unsuitable Job,* Gray's first client, Sir Ronald Callender, says to her, "Eighteen days ago my son hanged himself. I want you to find out why. Can you do that?" (39). In *Skull,* James seems to want us to replace this stark request with something on the order of, "Two days ago my cat ran away. I want you to find her. Can you do that?" And with Gray's first case in *Unsuitable Job,* she carefully informs her client, "We have a fair-play clause. If I decide at any stage of the investigation that I'd rather not go on with it, you are entitled to any information I have gained up to that point. If I decide to withhold it from you, then I make no charge for the work already done" (39). It is difficult to imagine circumstances under which the Gray of *Skull* would feel it necessary to tell her clients of the agency's fair-play clause, and this is in itself an indication of how trivial its activities have become. It is a commonplace of mystery and detective fiction analysis that one measure of the stature of a detective is the seriousness of the cases he or she is asked to solve. For this reason, the usual crimes investigated are murder and large-scale theft, and a detective who specializes in finding missing persons is far above one who specializes in finding missing dogs and cats (unless of course they are jeweled dogs and cats along the lines of the falcon in *The Maltese Falcon*).

I have argued elsewhere that James's male detective, Adam Dalgliesh, is a developing character who becomes more complex and more realistic over time. On the basis of the two novels featuring her female detective, Cordelia Gray, exactly the opposite seems to be true, with a once-realistic character who responded believably to her circumstances becoming flat, simplistic, and unconvincing. It is difficult to understand why P.D. James, having created such a strong figure in the Cordelia Gray of *Unsuitable Job,* chose to undermine and domesticate that figure in *Skull.* James has said that while she considers herself to be a feminist "in the sense that I like and admire women very much," she is not "in sympathy with the more extreme factions of Women's Lib" (Bakerman 57). It may be that after Gray's initial appearance James found this female hero, who takes as her talismans guns and leather, a character who is too extreme. Perhaps in domesticating Cordelia Gray in *The Skull Beneath the Skin,* James sought to correct the record, to emphasize in the revised character James's own cautious, qualified view of feminism. Whatever James's reasons, as someone who identified strongly with Cordelia Gray in her first incarnation, I was very disappointed in her the second time around. I want to believe that a woman can move from outsider to insider, can at least create a place for herself in the world of insiders, without having to betray her experience, her vision of the world she has come from, of how demeaning and limiting that world was and is. I believe that those of us lucky enough to have moved from one world to another must hold on to the sense of where we began so that we can act as mentors and can help one another find opportunity and at least some semblance of equality in the world of the white Anglo-Saxon patriarchy.

Works Cited

Bakerman, Jane S. "Interview with P.D. James." *Armchair Detective* 10 (1977): 55+.

James, P.D. *The Skull Beneath the Skin.* 1982. London: Sphere, 1988.

——. *An Unsuitable Job for a Woman.* 1972. New York: Warner, 1987.

Kotker, Joan G. "P.D. James's Adam Dalgliesh Series." *In the Beginning: First Novels in Mystery Series.* Ed. Mary Jean DeMarr. Bowling Green, OH: Bowling Green State University Popular Press, 1995.

Katherine V. Forrest:
Writing Kate Delafield for Us

Lois A. Marchino

Los Angeles Police Detective Kate Delafield is not revealed to us by circumstantial evidence: she is a strong, hard-working homicide detective whose lesbianism is the most significant aspect of her personal life. The four detective novels which feature Delafield directly involve gay and lesbian characters and cover a wide range of gay and lesbian issues. Although Delafield herself becomes an increasingly active member of the lesbian community, she remains officially closeted on her job because she has seen the pervasive mistreatment of other homosexual officers. Katherine V. Forrest—the best-selling author of the world's largest publisher of lesbian titles—creates in Kate Delafield a lesbian protagonist who engages our interest and whose cases address our concerns. Kate Delafield is written for us.

Forrest has said, "I don't have any confusion in my mind about who my audience is. I'm a lesbian writer and I write for a lesbian audience and I don't care if anyone else reads my books" (qtd. in Sosna, n.p.). Refreshing as this attitude may be to lesbian readers, it does not convey the entire scope of Forrest's influence. One can say that Forrest writes for (on behalf of) lesbians as much as she writes for (to) them. Forrest emphasizes issues that affect gay males as well as lesbians and by implication addresses discrimination against any individual or group. And indeed her novels are now read by many who are neither lesbian nor gay. The "us" for whom Forrest writes, then, is potentially a very wide range of readers.

Katherine Virginia Forrest (born in 1939) is a senior editor at Naiad Press in Tallahassee, Florida, where she prefers to publish her works rather than through mainstream publishers, though certainly her popularity makes her highly marketable. Along with Barbara Grier, head of Naiad, she has had immense influence on other contemporary lesbian writers through encouragement and example. She has been an enduring role model for writers of lesbian detective fiction, most notably Claire McNab, whose Detective Inspector Carol Ashton faces similar conflicts between her private life and her position on the Sydney, Australia, police force. Forrest publishes other types of fiction as well, and it is in part because of this previous reputation that she has become the best-known writer of lesbian mysteries among lesbian readers almost from the instant her first mystery, *Amateur City*, was published in 1984. The Kate Delafield series has been widely acclaimed by reviewers in lesbian periodicals. And although publications aimed exclusively toward gay males do not regularly review lesbian works, both Barbara Grier and Forrest agree that a sizeable portion of the readership for lesbian books is composed of gay men, in part, they believe, because of the romantic sensibility in lesbian novels (McDonald 45).

In his critical guide *Gay and Lesbian Characters and Themes in Mystery Novels*, Anthony Slide opens his relatively lengthy entry on Forrest by calling her "one of the best of lesbian mystery writers, and one whose novels can easily appeal to a mainstream audience" (54). The series is in fact increasingly appreciated by mainstream readers. Forrest's third Kate Delafield mystery, *The Beverly Malibu*, was Naiad's first mystery hardcover release, and *Murder by Tradition* the second; to date Forrest remains nearly the only Naiad author to be published in hardback. This not only attests to Forrest's popularity but adds to it, since hardcover books are more readily available in libraries and usually much more widely reviewed in trade magazines than are softcover editions. Mainstream reviewers are generally favorable in their comments, though some caution against recommending them for public school libraries because of the explicit lesbian sex scenes. Scholarly critics of women's detective fiction also generally praise Forrest.

Because of its quality, *Amateur City* was chosen as the first women's offering of Century Book Club, the first book club specifically for the gay and lesbian reader. *Murder at the Nightwood Bar* was produced as a feature film directed by Tim Hunter. Both *The Beverly Malibu* and *Murder by Tradition* won the Lambda Literary Award for best gay or lesbian mystery of the year for their respective years of publication. The Lambda is the highest literary award from the gay and lesbian community, sponsored by Lambda Rising in Washington, D.C., and its periodical the *Lambda Book Report*. *Murder by Tradition* is generally considered the finest novel in the series, and as the *Library Journal* review puts it, this "sizzling" courtroom drama "should quash any doubts concerning Forrest's abilities as a mystery writer, mainstream or otherwise" (Klett 141).

What, then, is it in Forrest's detective novels that attracts such a wide range of mystery readers, from lesbian and heterosexual women to gay and heterosexual males? There are those explicit sex scenes, to be discussed later, but the main reason is Forrest's ability to create entertaining and believable police procedurals which integrate plot, character, and theme. These elements function together to foreground lesbian and gay issues and also to address other overtly political issues such as homophobia, sexism, racism, ageism, body image, sexual harassment, AIDS, child molestation, and the lasting effects of the McCarthy witch hunts. Forrest's fundamental theme is human rights.

Like all writers who understand the challenges of multiple discrimination—in Forrest's case and that of many of her readers, "woman" and "lesbian"—Forrest forces us to face the reality of living in a still misogynist and homophobic culture. "Gaybasher," the term that startles Kate Delafield in *Murder by Tradition* when she realizes it applies to the murder of young Teddie Crawford, an openly gay man, is a term that has a literal, brutal referentiality, unlike the diluted connotation of "malebashing," ostensibly done by women making sharp comments about men. Gaybashing encompasses the verbal but most frequently manifests itself in physical violence. Gaybashing is broken bones and beat-up bodies. Gaybashing is bloody, as is Teddie's dead body with its thirty-nine stab wounds, wounds which still pour out their blood "in crimson gushes" when the homicide officers move the body (32). Blood becomes the dominant motif of the novel and the word "blood" or some variant ("bloody," "bleeding," "blood-soaked") appears at least 135 times. Forensic expert Charlotte Mead studies the blood-spatter patterns around the scene of the crime and from her evidence Kate is able to deduce and demonstrate that Teddie never held the knife, much less initiated any attack. It is "the evidence about the blood especially" that most convinces the jury that Kyle Jensen is guilty of murder in the first degree (271).

In the courtroom, the psychology of Jensen's obsessive and repeated stabbing attack is discussed largely in terms of his hatred of what he calls "fags" and the clear evidence that he knew from the start that his victim was gay because Teddie had been obvious and open about his sexual preference. But outside the courtroom, Forrest has forensic expert Charlotte Mead graphically allude to the knife used by the murderer as the psychological equivalent of his penis. As Kate Delafield knows, "A familiar tenet among law enforcement professionals held that multiple stabbing was a sign of sexual pathology" (18). Jensen, who is much bigger and stronger than Teddie, had picked up Teddie at a bar frequented by gays but later claims he was sickened by Teddie's homosexual manners and killed to defend himself from Teddie's alleged sexual advances. In doing so, he forced Teddie face down on the floor, straddled his body, and stabbed him in the back repeatedly; Jensen's jeans and shorts become saturated with blood. Clearly we are meant to see both the pathology and the connection between hatred of homosexuals and persons who are insecure in their own sexual identity. Linda Foster, the prosecuting attorney, suggests Jensen was killing the homosexual in himself, and Kate reflects, "Somebody once said that the hater actually longs for the object of his hatred" (104). In *Murder at the Nightwood Bar*, a young lesbian is repeatedly bashed with an aluminum baseball bat, bludgeoned to death by her own mother. Young Dory Quillin, who had become a prostitute for a circle of businessmen, had been sexually abused by her father for many years, and she was planning to expose the evidence of his guilt in other assaults on children. Her mother, in complete denial, cannot allow that to happen. A religious fanatic, she has claimed not to believe Dory; but her main obsession is the horror that her daughter is a lesbian. Again Forrest knows this plot scenario is not as improbable as we would like it to be. A recent report issued by the American Psychological Association blames "widely accepted prejudice" for making gay and lesbian youth more vulnerable to violent victimization, and it notes that over half of the violence is perpetrated by family members. Another study shows that 46 percent of teenagers reporting violent physical assaults said the assault was related to their sexual orientation. Of these, 61 percent reported that the violence occurred within the family (Knorr 1).

In contrast to the innocent victims of these two novels, the victims in *Amateur City* and *The Beverly Malibu* are despicable men who abuse and betray those around them. As usual, these novels quickly move to Kate's arrival at the murder scene, and Kate learns there is no sympathy for the deceased. In *Amateur City* the dead boss had sexually harassed both female and male employees; on the day he is murdered they go to lunch together and drink a toast to whoever killed him. His wife, also abused, is equally happy that he is dead. Reader sympathy is not directed toward the perpetrator, since Kate fears he may kill again to cover up his impulsive act, but we are presented with the imperative need to change the social climate that allows an employer or anyone in a position of power to harass and abuse others.

The Beverly Malibu describes an even more long-standing resentment against an unlikable victim. Kate's Thanksgiving Day is interrupted by the grisly murder of seventy-three-year-old Owen Sinclair, a former film director, whose handcuffed body is found in the bedroom of his apartment at the edge of Beverly Hills. The other fifteen or so residents in the Beverly Malibu apartment building are immediate suspects, since all of them had attended the party at which Sinclair apparently ingested strychnine. Kate's investigation reveals that nearly everyone had reasons to dislike him, from his insufferably loud music to his stealing filmscripts and claiming them as his own. Even worse, he had been a "friendly witness" (an informer) for the House Un-American Activities Committee (HUAC) in the 1950s and he turned over to the committee virtually everyone he had ever met, destroying careers and ruining lives. His death, and that of another resident, Dudley Kincaid (whose murder interrupts Kate's Christmas Day), are both directly tied to these events of three decades earlier. Forrest gives credit to Lillian Hellman's *Scoundrel Time* for vividly describing the terrors of that era. Forrest provides a history lesson for readers unfamiliar with the sufferings of those brought before the HUAC, and in the process she provides parallels with contemporary attitudes toward gays and lesbians. The days of "witch hunts" are not over.

It is no surprise that the murderer in *The Beverly Malibu* is one of the victims of the HUAC era, a woman whose family life was shattered. Driven mad over the loss of her husband and daughter, she describes holiday seasons afterward as "particularly hideous," and she chooses to avenge herself through holiday murders (259). She does so not just for herself, but on behalf of all the innocent victims who suffered at the hands of the HUAC. The novel ends with Kate helping to foil a plot by the murderer to kill ex-President Nixon, one of the "hoodlums" involved with Senator Joseph McCarthy and the others who chose to use their power to punish suspected communists, homosexuals, and anyone else they considered unacceptable (264). One character says of those days: "Treachery everywhere you turn, the feeling of constantly being hunted—and all because of your beliefs" (258). Kate responds by reflecting about the United States: "a country where it's not supposed to happen," but in her thoughts she adds, "being singled out and persecuted is what being gay or lesbian has always been about . . ." (ellipsis Forrest, 258). Yet despite her sympathy with the perpetrator's delayed impulse to retaliate against those she sees as the true betrayers of liberty, Kate speaks out against adopting the mind set of the oppressor: "You wanted to know how I came to be a police officer," she tells one of the women involved with the case. "I do what I can to live in a civilized world. Vengeance isn't my job, or yours, or [the killer's]" (260).

The irony of Kate's situation here and throughout the series is a central irony in the lives of most gays and lesbians historically and in the world now: working within the law but being considered outlaws. In many of the fifty states today homosexuality is still illegal. In some it is not criminal to "be" homosexual, but to perform homosexual acts is. Even with a more enlightened presidential administration the United States military policy forbids those in the service to reveal their same-sex orientation by word or deed. And beyond the law itself remain many religious proscriptions, as personified in the Pope, whose repeated denunciations of homosexuality he considers to be God's view. There is social stigmatizing; and silencing of speech and art; and discrimination in housing, parenting, marrying; and on and on. The vigilante actions against gays and lesbians continue. They continue indeed, in part, because lesbians and gays have become much more visible in society and successful in political action. As with women and minority groups such as African Americans, strides toward equality are still met with opponents who react with increased hostility.

Exactly why anyone should be hostile toward gays and lesbians—most of whom are like Kate Delafield, at least as honest and hard working and compassionate as most heterosexuals—remains a conundrum. Presumably it relates to the construction and continuation of patriarchal power; by its very existence same-sex love challenges traditional roles and the hierarchy of those roles—who controls, who makes the rules. Like women, homosexuals are represented in every race, class, and age group. There is no official party line, no total unanimity of views or political awareness. Many still acknowledge their sexual orientation only in very selected situations. Yet by virtue of not playing by the dominant rules—by not being heterosexual—all lesbians and gays implicitly challenge somebody's fears, evidently. But it is too late for the opposition; we must assume and work as though human rights will expand and prevail. Or, as Jill Johnston boldly put it in *Lesbian Nation: The Feminist Solution*, "That awful life of having to choose between being a criminal or going straight was over. We were going to legitimize ourselves as criminals!" (Johnston 97).

Kate Delafield is no outlaw or criminal except in the sense of larger social attitudes towards homosexuality. She has no personal guilt or regret over her erotic attraction to women, but neither is she an overt radical or public spokesperson demanding immediate change. If anything, current lesbian readers may see Kate as too conservative, too willing to hide her private life from her professional situation, too willing to let hostile and antigay/lesbian remarks remain undefended. Kate herself understands this uneasy position, and as the series develops she becomes less tolerant of the social/legal discrimination against herself and against those she increasingly acknowledges as her sisters and brothers in the lesbian/gay struggle.

Kate is in many ways both representative and exemplar of contemporary lesbian consciousness. Forrest creates her protagonist as a woman who emerged as a lesbian before there was an available community for her. Born in 1946, Kate says that her upbringing and influences were from the fifties, precisely that repressive reactionary era of the HUAC hearings. As Sally Munt points out in "The Inverstigators: Lesbian Crime Fiction," Kate's cultural background is lesbian rather than lesbian-feminist. Her parents have long since died and she has no siblings. Growing tall and strong before other girls her age, she considered herself an outsider. While a student at the University of Michigan in Ann Arbor, she went with a friend to a lesbian bar in Detroit and was angry and humiliated by the furtive atmosphere, the distorted role-playing of "butch" and "femme," the voyeuristic stares of heterosexual couples. After she met her long-term lover, Anne, she never went to a bar again until a homicide case brings her to the Nightwood Bar. She is both surprised and pleased by the Nightwood; places like that simply did not exist when she was younger.

Actually very little information is given about Kate's earlier years, perhaps to reemphasize her role as a loner who has learned to take care of herself, or perhaps Forrest wants to move beyond the coming out story which has understandably dominated lesbian fiction, the "how I came to recognize my sexuality and found a woman to love and found others like us" story. This lack of information is also effective as a symbol of the invisibility of lesbianism not only during Kate's early years but for centuries before her. Like the colonization of an indigenous people, those who are subsumed by a hostile culture may deliberately "forget" the bad times, or choose not to dwell on them. If they are denied a written history as well, it is little wonder that when they manage to break through these barriers, they speak and write of present accomplishments and look forward rather than back to the silenced past. For many readers, especially those of or around the baby-boomer generation, this recognizing/being recognized speaking/writing "being out" came in conjunction with the women's liberation movement which began in the late 1960s and has continued. Today we are aware of such pioneers as Del Martin and Phyllis Lyon whose magazine *The Ladder* instilled a sense of lesbian pride in the 1950s, even if only to a small readership. The 1969 Stonewall riot, in which gays resisted the standard round-up of gay bar patrons by New York police, marked a turning point in gay/lesbian cultural history and became a major rallying cry for respect and civil rights.

Meanwhile, Kate Delafield (whose history fits the 1939 birth date of her creator better than the implied year of 1946), recalls her thrill at finding Ann Bannon's 1950s pulp fiction featuring Beebo Brinker in Greenwich Village; Beebo was at least an openly homosexual character who enjoyed herself. On Kate's twenty-first birthday in 1967 she made her one visit to the bar in Detroit, the bar which to Kate "was too much like the place which housed her grandmother—a ghetto of the exiled, of the classified hopeless" (*Amateur City* 34). (We learn nothing further about her grandmother.) Kate leaves the university during her senior year, joining the Marine Corps and serving a year in Vietnam. In retrospect she sees this enlistment as "her first significant defiance of a peer group which had dictated too many aspects of her life. And four years later she had met Anne—and in the precious years afterward her life had expanded in meaning and impact. Never again had she set foot in a lesbian bar . . ." (ellipsis Forrest, *Amateur City* 34).

When Kate makes her entrance in the series at the opening of chapter 2 in *Amateur City*, it is February 8, probably 1983 (the exact year is noted in the subsequent three novels as Kate writes down the date and time of her arrival at the homicide scene). Kate is now an eleven-year veteran of the L.A.P.D., having joined the force in 1972, around the same time she started living with Anne, about the year she quit smoking. Anne, who had been her monogamous partner for twelve years, has been dead for five months, killed in a fiery car crash. In the following novels Kate always mentions how long it has been since this devastating blow changed her life and she always compares her feelings for other women to her relationship with Anne. In *Amateur City* she meets Ellen O'Neill. Kate thinks that Ellen looks a lot like Anne (though later she admits few real similarities exist) and immediately assumes she is a lesbian.

Nicole Décuré, in her close study of Kate in the first two novels, chides Forrest for having all her lesbian characters "recognize a lesbian at first glance," because in appearance or action "the masculine points to the lesbian" (273). Décuré's criticism is a trifle unfair. Kate Delafield knows there is no one set appearance for gays or lesbians. And besides—and not to be contradictory or to claim 100 percent accuracy—lesbians often do pride themselves on their ability to spot kindred souls and are certainly more likely to notice each other than non-lesbians are. Décuré goes on to say, "To Kate Delafield, a lesbian is born, not made. She has no more control over her sexuality than over the colour of her eyes or skin. How that comes about, goddess knows, as one of the characters likes to say. It is just one of those articles of faith that enables homosexuals of both sexes to feel less guilty about their sexual preference. A lesbian is predetermined" (273). Yes, Kate does think it is "nature," but Décuré should not assume lesbians think there is anything to feel guilty about. It is worth mentioning such examples from Décuré because her essay is representative of interest in Forrest's works and suggests the kinds of topics the novels raise. Lesbians—and others— repeatedly explore such issues as how and when sexual diversity is determined, what signals sexual orientation to others, which clues are "fashions" in a given time and place, and so forth. Commentary on Forrest's novels (or any literary work) also demonstrates again that just as there are "feminisms" rather than a monolithic "feminism," so too no one speaks for all lesbians or, indeed, can even know who is lesbian or precisely what lesbian means. As with most words, definition becomes more complex the more one considers the term, and it is not always easy to decide what constitutes "lesbian." Similarly, the terms used change; Catherine R. Stimpson in "Zero Degree Deviancy: The Lesbian Novel in English," notes that "the first citation for lesbianism as a female passion in *The Shorter Oxford English Dictionary* is 1908; for 'sapphism' 1890" (365). "Lesbian" is not a term that all women-identified-women today like or use. Forrest wisely chooses not to define "lesbian" but to use it in a positive sense, attempting to create a group solidarity among her lesbian characters and among her lesbian readers. And—an advantage of recognizing others—Kate never mistakenly falls for a heterosexual; her love interests are with women who already acknowledge themselves as lovers of women.

Forrest is clear about presenting Kate Delafield's relationships with her lovers as meaningful and supportive. Kate's brief period of intimacy with Ellen O'Neill is important both to Kate and to Ellen. Kate needs to feel someone cares for her and expresses a need for reassurance about her attractiveness at this point after Anne's death. Ellen needs personal as well as professional guidance and comforting. She may be in danger from the murderer, and the woman she lives with, economics professor Stephanie Hale, is away at a conference. In addition, Ellen and Stephanie are on the verge of splitting up, since Stephanie wants a "wife" to help write her next book but Ellen wants greater independence. To Ellen and Kate the situation seems right and the attraction between them is strong. They both gain from sharing intimacy. Ellen is able to more clearly understand the problems with Stephanie and realizes that together they can come to terms with their conflicts. Kate feels reconnected with her sense of self. Kate and Ellen remain friendly and grateful for their loving time together.

Similarly, in *Murder at the Nightwood Bar*, there is mutual respect and attraction between Kate and Andrea, one of the women she meets when she is gathering information about Dory Quillin's death in her van outside the Nightwood. The year is 1985; Kate is thirty-nine. The brief time Kate and Andrea spend together is healing and comforting as well as erotic; in this instance it is Andrea who most needs reassurance, since she has recently had a radical mastectomy and she has not been able to deal with her lover Bev's or her own reaction to the operation. After being with Kate, Andrea is better able to accept herself and work out things with her estranged partner. Again, Kate uncomplainingly accepts the situation for what it is. In discussing the love situations for Kate in these first two books in the series, Nicole Décuré concludes, "Like many a male detective, Kate's sexual life is confined to one-night stands, at long intervals in time. This is perhaps why we get so many details in *the* sex scene of each book. Katherine V. Forrest has to make the most of it" (Décuré 273).

In *Murder at the Nightwood Bar* Kate does establish a solid friendship with Maggie, the owner of the Nightwood, and that friendship will continue to develop and be important to Kate in the subsequent novels. Her love-relationships change too. In *The Beverly Malibu*, set in 1988, Kate is attracted to an older woman, Paula, one of the residents in the apartment building, but Paula considers herself a one-woman woman and wants to remain true to the memory of her long-term companion, now deceased. Ironically it is Kate's homophobic partner, Ed Taylor, who calls Kate's attention to Paula's beautiful young niece, Aimee, who has already noticed Kate and makes the first advances. Their love-making seems to Kate truly extraordinary, and they are still together in *Murder by Tradition*, set in 1989. With Maggie's encouragement, Kate is learning to trust her much younger lover with the rough details of her worklife, and despite their age difference the relationship moves toward a more equal partnership than Kate has ever experienced. Her situation with Anne had been in the older tradition of Kate as "husband" and Anne as "wife," but social patterns are changing, including Kate's developing strong friendships with Maggie and some of the other regulars at the Nightwood Bar, where *Murder by Tradition* ends with a victory celebration after the trial.

Kate's sexual intimacy with other women is a vital part of her life, and Ellen, Andrea, and Aimee are characters interwoven into the plots of the novels and their connections with Kate are plausible. There really isn't much point in creating a lesbian protagonist and then never letting her have sex. Forrest provides one or two or three explicit sex scenes in each novel. A sample, from *Murder by Tradition*: "She kissed her throat, exploring until she felt the pulse beat; she pressed her lips hard against it. Aimee uttered a sound, a vibration under Kate's mouth. Kate lowered herself onto her, groaning with the bliss of Aimee's warm nakedness everywhere melding into hers. Kissing her, she pushed a thigh between Aimee's legs. . . . For long moment she breathed in a woman smell that seemed to go beyond woman to creation itself" (ellipsis mine, 95-97). Yes, ellipsis mine, which is probably how I would write it if I were writing the scene, but Forrest invariably goes on for three or four pages, and more graphically, so no one can ask the unimaginative old question,

"But what do lesbians do?" and no one can pretend the author means something else.

Including explicit scenes of love-making and sensuality in lesbian fiction serves many purposes, and it is difficult to assess which messages the writer hopes will be sent or which are received. Literary tastes and sensibilities vary, and the reaction of readers varies. As a student said of the love scenes in *Murder at the Nightwood Bar*, I don't think I should want them in a detective story, but I certainly read them. Reaction also varies from one text to another, or from the first to the second or third reading of the same text. Perhaps it is the variety of views about love and sex (both from author and reader) that is important: something for everyone. Or perhaps it is the assumption by writers and publishers that sex sells. One can almost hear Barbara Grier at Naiad telling authors their manuscripts will be accepted if they throw in a few torrid sex scenes (in fact, I once asked Grier that, and she said, "Of course!").

Writing directly about sex has been largely taboo for women, and it is not easy to create a vocabulary, style, and tone that conveys the passion and joy of two women loving. In Doris Lessing's *The Golden Notebook* writer Anna Wulf says, "Sex. The difficulty of writing about sex, for women, is that sex is best when not thought about, not analysed. Women deliberately choose not to think about technical sex. They get irritable when men talk technically, it's out of self-preservation: they want to preserve the spontaneous emotion that is essential for their satisfaction. Sex is essentially emotional for women" (214). To put it another way, the experience of sexuality at its most intense goes beyond words; that is one of its attractions. As with any mystical illumination, it cannot be directly revealed in words, but must be represented through symbol and form. Still, since most of the love scenes by women writers in the past have been expressed through such allusion and encoding (for example, in Djuna Barnes's novel *Nightwood*, to cite the reference that provides Forrest's name for her bar), it is understandable that current women writers often choose again to break the patterns.

Readers of detective fiction who prefer fewer distractions from the mystery plot might remind ourselves that in Forrest and other lesbian mystery writers, sexuality is not only a major component of characterization but also a statement of humanist values, and a lesbian feminist revisioning that includes seeing the ongoing process of development of self always in relation to others. In the Bildungsroman aspects of the lesbian novel, the female protagonist assumes her role in the wider world, challenging the public/private dichotomy.

With all the current emphasis on sexuality in women's mystery writing, we might well consider Bobbie Ann Mason's analysis of Nancy

Drew in her excellent study *The Girl Sleuth*. Mason reminds us that Nancy Drew existed in a world which affirmed "a double standard for female sexuality: attention to beauty and clamps on virginity" (65). In the original series, those famous blue hardbacks starting in 1929, Nancy solved more than fifty mysteries, most of them, as Mason wryly notes, "in the summer of the eighteenth year" (49). Nancy is "an eternal girl, a stage which is a false ideal for women of our time" (75). The mysteries, Mason concludes, "are a substitute for sex, since sex is the greatest mystery of all for adolescents" (63).

The widespread focus on sex in current detective novels (both homosexual and heterosexual) suggests that sex is a mystery not only to adolescents. But lesbian detectives have certainly grown beyond being girl sleuths, and the ideals they represent are suggested as much by their romantic attachments as by their solving the crime. As Nichols and Thompson say in *Silk Stalkings: When Women Write of Murder*, women writers tend "to focus less on the actual crime and more on the relationships of the characters involved with the case" (xv). Nichols and Thompson conclude: "Human nature in all its permutations is the foundation of the mystery metaphor" (xvi). Or, as Maureen Reddy says in *Sisters in Crime*, it is no coincidence that the lesbian detective novel is "the one that most directly challenges generic conventions by making explicit the social critique that is more covert in most other crime novels," and that lesbian crime novels "more often than other women's mysteries address issues of race and class as well, illuminating the conjunction of sex, race, and class oppression" (16).

Reddy acknowledges that some of the sex scenes in lesbian mysteries seem gratuitous, artificial, and annoying (though she does not cite Forrest in this category), but she also reminds us that "the feminist crime novel is still in its youth, and so aesthetic judgments seem premature" (17). We do, in fact, tend to forget just how recent is this now popular category of "feminist sleuths," and how very recent is the lesbian sleuth. *Gay and Lesbian Characters and Themes in Mystery Novels* lists the 1982 publication of Vicki P. McConnell's *Mrs. Porter's Letters* (Naiad Press) as the first lesbian mystery novel. One might arguably give that distinction to a few other books, but the point is well taken; it is not a subgenre with a long literary history. Vicki McConnell went on to publish two other mysteries featuring her pioneering amateur sleuth Nyla Wade, but by that time she was joined by others, and by now there are numerous writers (both lesbian and non) who include lesbian characters. There are at least thirty self-identified lesbian writers who have ongoing lesbian sleuths in a mystery series, several with four or five books.

This amazing bursting forth of lesbian detective fiction clearly suggests that writers did not just create readers; a sizeable audience was waiting. In her article "On Becoming a Lesbian Reader," Alison Hennegan speaks of her experience of reading "my way through endless heterosexual novels which never seemed to acknowledge my perspective on the world" (175).

> Although I didn't know it at the time, my rage and perplexity as an adolescent reader were shared by thousands of other homosexual women and men who loved books too well to let them go on lying. The Movement which we made later was primarily concerned with truth. 'Coming out' was both a tactical and moral imperative. And we made writing "come out" as well as people. . . . Our growing visibility within the reading population at large persuaded mainstream publishers that it was worth identifying and meeting our needs, persuaded some of our own number that specifically gay and lesbian presses could survive. (188-89)

Catherine Stimpson lists the larger socioeconomic reasons for lesbian literature's appearance in strength, naming a confluence of forces: "the women's movement, more flexible attitudes toward marriage (so often contrasted favorably to the putative anarchy of homosexual relations), the 'modernization of sex,' which encourages a rational, tolerant approach to the complexities of eros, and the growing entrance of more women into the public labor force, which gives a financial autonomy inseparable from genuine sexual independence" (360).

Stimpson also comments, "The continued strength of literary form can stand for the continued strength of the larger community's norms" (363). Thus reader(s), writer(s), and text(s) have a profoundly inter-related mutualism. Forrest and other writers need a readership which supports and buys their books; readers need to know lesbian writers/ lesbian texts are available as part of the ongoing development of both self and community.

Popular culture has always been a guide to what is important in a society, and this remains true of contemporary detective fiction. Feminist and lesbian-feminist mystery writers have not appropriated the male detective in fiction as much as reappropriated the autonomy that should always have been ours. As Craig and Cadogan say in *The Lady Investigates*, the woman detective embodies "two qualities often disallowed for women in the past: the power of action and practical intelligence" (246). To this the lesbian detective adds the power of loving women. Her loving becomes an emblem for living with compassion and hope. Like other writers of lesbian detective novels,

Forrest gives us strong emotional exchanges between lovers rather than casual, violent, or exploitative sex. She shows the strength of supportive female friendships and provides positive models validating various choices for women.

Kate Delafield is no impossibly perfect superhero, nor is she a finished, fully evolved character (Naiad plans to publish the fifth in the series in 1996), but she is an important figure in contemporary women's literature, especially to the extent she represents the still emerging voices of the audience(s) for whom Katherine V. Forrest writes. In an ideal society there would be little need for detectives or for sexual labels, but in the current world and the world of novels, we could propose a salute: To Kate Delafield and her sister sleuths: long may they live and love.

Works Cited

Craig, Patricia, and Mary Cadogan. *The Lady Investigates: Women Detectives and Spies in Fiction.* New York: St. Martin's, 1981.

Décuré, Nicole. "From the Closet to the Bleachers: Kate Delafield: Portrait of a Lesbian as a 'Lady Cop.'" *Women Studies International Forum* 15 (1992) New York: 267-79.

Forrest, Katherine V. *Amateur City.* Tallahassee: Naiad, 1984.

——. *Murder at the Nightwood Bar.* Tallahassee: Naiad, 1987.

——. *The Beverly Malibu.* Tallahassee: Naiad, 1990.

——. *Murder by Tradition.* Tallahassee: Naiad, 1991.

Hennegan, Alison. "On Becoming a Lesbian Reader." *Sweet Dreams: Sexuality, Gender and Popular Fiction.* Ed. Susannah Radstone. London: Lawrence and Wishart, 1988. 165-90.

Johnston, Jill. *Lesbian Nation: The Feminist Solution.* New York: Simon and Schuster, 1973.

Klett, Rex E. Rev. of *Murder by Tradition*, by Katherine V. Forrest. *Library Journal* 116 (July 1991): 141.

Knorr, Christopher. "Study: Most Violence Against Gay Youth Occurs in Home." *Windy City Times: Chicago's Gay and Lesbian Newsweekly* 2 Sept. 1993: 1.

Lessing, Doris. *The Golden Notebook.* New York: Knopf, 1962.

Mason, Bobbie Ann. *The Girl Sleuth: A Feminist Guide.* Old Westbury, NY: Feminist Press, 1975.

McDonald, Sharon. "Katherine Forrest, A Passionate, Gutsy Storyteller." *The Advocate* 2 Oct. 1984: 45-46.

Munt, Sally. "The Inverstigators: Lesbian Crime Fiction." *Sweet Dreams: Sexuality, Gender and Popular Fiction*. Ed. Susannah Radstone. London: Lawrence and Wishart, 1988.

Nichols, Victoria, and Susan Thompson. *Silk Stalkings: When Women Write of Murder*. Berkeley: Black Lizard, 1988.

Reddy, Maureen T. *Sisters in Crime: Feminism and the Crime Novel*. New York: Continuum, 1988.

Slide, Anthony. *Gay and Lesbian Characters and Themes in Mystery Novels: A Critical Guide to Over 500 Works in English*. Jefferson, NC: McFarland, 1993.

Sosna, Laurie. "An Interview: Katherine Forrest." [Fresno, CA] *Newsletter* Jan. 1989: N. pag.

Stimpson, Catherine R. "Zero Degree Deviancy: The Lesbian Novel in English." *Homosexual Themes in Literary Studies*. Ed. Wayne R. Dynes and Stephen Donaldson. New York: Garland, 1992. 349-69. The essay first appeared in *Critical Inquiry* 8 (1981).

"Collaring the Other Fellow's Property": Feminism Reads Dorothy L. Sayers

Elizabeth A. Trembley

I began my studies of Dorothy L. Sayers's work as part of an investigation into how women detectives developed. However, my interest focused on Sayers and her female hero, Harriet Vane, when my research revealed an overwhelming negative response to Sayers's handling of Harriet from female and "feminist" critics.[1] Though critics have discussed detective fiction since the Golden Age of the 1920s, those interested in Dorothy L. Sayers have tended to focus on her series detective, Lord Peter Wimsey. Prior to 1970, little, if any, mention is made of Harriet, except as a foil for Lord Peter. It is the critical discussions that appeared between 1970 and 1985 that I will examine here.

Discussion of Harriet as a valuable and complex character in her own right begins with the growth of feminist criticism: a new focus on female authors and their female characters and the tales these authors tell about the world. While this political orientation fostered most of the thoughtful consideration of Harriet Vane, it also produced the most violently negative response to her. Feminist critics' dissatisfaction with Sayers's treatment of Harriet Vane focuses on the events at the end of *Gaudy Night* and throughout *Busman's Honeymoon*—Harriet's acceptance of Lord Peter Wimsey's marriage proposal and their consequent honeymoon. Critics who have not felt negatively toward Harriet throughout her adventures in *Strong Poison*, *Have His Carcase*, and the bulk of *Gaudy Night* find these final episodes disappointing and annoying. Why?

Critics with feminist leanings seem to feel that in her joining of Harriet Vane and Lord Peter Wimsey, Sayers betrayed the feminist design of the first three novels. In her 1980 study of three feminist detectives, Kathleen Gregory Klein devotes a third of her space to remarks on Harriet Vane; however, she makes no mention of the existence of *Busman's Honeymoon*. Other critics acknowledge the novel only to complain about the marriage, remarking on the apparent loss of Harriet's independence: Margot Peters and Agate Krouse claim that Harriet, "an intelligent, spirited, and successful professional writer, a woman who could be Wimsey's equal if not his superior . . . capitulates" (147-48) to Lord Peter, while Patricia Craig and Mary Cadogan agree that "the capitulation of dogged, self-reliant Harriet Vane is nothing if not complete" (188). Auerbach insists that in *Busman's Honeymoon* "Harriet's gain of love is a loss of life and power" (193) as she "obliterates herself systematically in order to fulfill his [Peter's] needs" (194). Eventually Harriet becomes "all bosom enfolding him away from the march of time and consequences of death" (194). Craig and Cadogan seem to agree: "Harriet's purpose in this book is to keep him cheerful and reassured" (188).

Such critical dissatisfaction with Sayers's treatment of Harriet Vane in *Gaudy Night* and *Busman's Honeymoon* stems from an essential misreading of the materials that the author provides in all four of the completed Harriet Vane novels. Many critics work from a basic assumption derived from the earlier texts (*Strong Poison*, *Have His Carcase*, and most of *Gaudy Night*) that Dorothy L. Sayers began her Harriet Vane novels with a feminist agenda which she later abandoned. This assumption leads to the primary reason for critical disappointment: the perception that Harriet Vane began her existence as a feminist heroine, then sadly grew more conventional over time, finally capitulating to Peter in marriage. In identifying Harriet's marriage to Peter as a capitulation or abandonment of female self-sufficiency, critics indicate their dismay at Sayers's changes to Harriet's character. Familiar with a tradition of women writers treating their heroines in precisely this disappointing fashion, they see the same thing happening again: Sayers's potential to create a vibrant feminist character disintegrates with Harriet's final conventionality.[2]

In this article I will illustrate how both of these responses to the last novel are skewed by false assumptions about the earlier texts, misreadings motivated by the critics' own agendas. First, I will argue against the idea that Sayers had a feminist agenda by illustrating her distaste for feminism; then I will argue that Sayers did not create Harriet Vane as an independent woman with feminist goals. Finally, I will suggest why feminists read the novels this way and identify another approach to the texts which explains more adequately Sayers's treatment of her heroine's destiny.

Before I begin with Sayers, I must clarify the term "feminism" which I have used so freely. Critics have already spent much time and effort trying to provide a universal definition of the term, as a quick perusal of recent feminist books or journals will prove, so I will attempt no such thing. The definition often seems to vary between individuals, and the term often carries connotations which do not apply to the woman wishing to call herself a feminist. For this reason, many women today concerned with social and economic inequality hesitate to call themselves feminists. Here, however, I hope to point out some of the basic beliefs that seem to underlie the broad spectrum of feminism as it exists today, so that I can better illustrate the differences in Dorothy L. Sayers's beliefs.

Elaine Showalter charts the history of feminism by dividing it into three distinct phases; Dorothy L. Sayers grew to maturity between the last two. Showalter identifies the era from 1880 to 1920 as the "Feminist Phase," a time when women rejected accommodating postures of femininity, used "literature to dramatize the ordeals of wronged womanhood . . . [and] redefined the woman artist's role in terms of recognition of responsibility to suffering sisters" (132). This phase of thinking began to change as women achieved the vote. The period after 1920 represents the "Female Phase," a time when women turned "to female experience as the source of autonomous art . . . representations of the formal Female Aesthetic . . . redefining and sexualizing external and internal experience" (139). Much of the feminism that has developed since then continues this trend, taking women as a special interest group, focusing either on woman as reader or woman as author of texts. However, because this new focus divides one segment of humanity from another and operates on a paradigm of privilege, Sayers opposed it.

Sayers believed that women's struggle with inequality rose from the social conception of women and men as utterly different beings. In "The Human-Not-Quite-Human," one of her two essays on women's rights, she explains this. "*Vir* is male and *Femina* is female: but *Homo* is male and female. . . . Man is always dealt with as both *Homo* and *Vir*, but Woman only as *Femina*" (116). Thus, Sayers felt that the women's movement, insofar as it tried to emphasize difference and to make *Femina* equal to *Vir*, was misguided and doomed. Such polarization could lead to dangerous ideological fervor. In a letter to Mrs. O.W. Campbell, Sayers warned that any special attitude, whether feminist, or National-Socialist, corrupted judgment.[3]

While her comparison of feminists to Nazis may seem harsh, it helps us understand Sayers's distaste for feminism. Her essays further help us understand her suspicion. "I was not sure I wanted to 'identify myself,' as the phrase goes, with feminism. . . . In fact, I think I went so far as to say that, under present conditions, an aggressive feminism might do more harm than good" ("Are Women Human?" 106). While Sayers clearly believed that society's treatment of women left much to be desired, she did not agree with the separatist approach to achieving equality.

What is repugnant to every human being is to be reckoned always as a member
of a class and not as an individual person . . . to assume that *all* one's tastes and
preferences have to be conditioned by the class to which one belongs. That has
been . . . the error into which feminist women are, perhaps, a little inclined to
fall about themselves. ("Are Women Human?" 107)

Sayers believed equality for women would come only when both men
and women stopped emphasizing the *Vir/Femina* difference and instead
concentrated on recognizing the *Homo*, or species, similarities among
males and females with no domination between them (letter to Miss
Dorothy M.E. Dawson). Women had not received such "human"
treatment and Sayers believed frustration with the situation had carried
feminists off in the wrong direction.

In reaction against the age-old slogan "woman is the weaker vessel," or the still
more offensive, "woman is a divine creature," we have, I think, allowed ourselves
to drift into asserting that "a woman is as good as a man," without always pausing
to think exactly what we mean by that. ("Are Women Human?" 107)

Sayers feared it sometimes meant that women behaved in ways she felt
were both foolish and undesirable simply to achieve equality with men.
    Clearly Sayers was as much concerned about the motives behind
the feminist movement as with the social changes it achieved. She felt
feminists should insist "not that every woman is, in virtue of her sex, as
strong, clever, artistic, level-headed, industrious and so forth as any man
that can be mentioned; but, that a woman is just as much an ordinary
human being as a man" ("Are Women Human?" 107). Women must ask
themselves, she cautioned, "is it something useful, convenient and
suitable to a human being as such? Or is it merely something
unnecessary to us, ugly, and adopted merely for the sake of collaring the
other fellow's property?" (109).
    One such standard adopted from the male social sphere is the
evaluation of a person based on his or her independence from others.
Even today, feminist critics who are attracted to Harriet's spunky
independence and tough resilience, and who mourn what they view as
the necessary loss of this independence when Harriet marries a wealthy
aristocrat, have taken this cue from a patriarchal society which valorizes
independence and self-sufficiency as the means to safety and power.
Even as modern feminists like Judi Roller proclaim that their mission is
to "suggest a need for a basic change and restructuring in Western
government, culture, and society" (6), they still evaluate a woman's
success in terms of traditional criteria. Western culture has long

encouraged its male members to seek individualism, providing opportunities and encouragement to grow toward self-sufficiency, while traditionally requiring women to remain dependent and undeveloped. "Men are to be independent, rational, achieving, competitive, success-oriented, tough, self-reliant, and aggressive. Women are to be emotional, nurturant, interpersonally-oriented, dependent, caring and intuitive" (Olds 7). Thus many feminists applaud women like Harriet Vane who exhibit such traditionally male characteristics as progressive. When, in *Busman's Honeymoon*, Harriet responds to Peter in a more traditionally feminine way, many critics view her behavior as regressive and counter to feminist development.

Sayers, as her essays and life proved, did not believe that nurturing interpersonal orientation or marriage necessarily had any negative effects on an individual's personal development. She discusses the question of marriage within the struggle for women's equality, asserting that "the time has now come to insist more strongly on each woman's— and indeed each man's—requirements as an individual person" ("Are Women Human?" 116). She outlines what she believes all people want: "interesting occupation, reasonable freedom for their pleasures, and a sufficient emotional outlet" (114). Sayers believed marriage was an integral requirement for happiness which some men achieved yet which no woman could: marriage without having to sacrifice occupation, pleasure, or emotions.

What woman really prefers a job to a home and family? Very few, I admit. It is unfortunate that they should so often have to make the choice. A man does not, as a rule, have to choose. . . . When it comes to a choice, then every man or woman has to choose as an individual human being and, like a human being, take the consequences. (10)

Though modern critics may think that reasonable occupation, pleasure, and emotional outlet can be achieved without marriage, Sayers did not think so. As her various biographies point out, marriage held top priority for Dorothy after she graduated from college, and she did not at all consider it detrimental to her own personal fight for social equality.

By stating that Sayers was not a feminist, I do not wish to give the impression that she thought women had no social problems or that she saw no reason for change. However, Sayers had her own vision of how the problems should be approached. In 1942, as she refused a request that she lead a women's crusade, Sayers offered her advice for the road women should take, saying only work brought equality and feminism implied inferiority (letter to Miss Dorothy M.E. Dawson). While Sayers clearly felt that society had for centuries mistreated and misrepresented women and that a struggle for equality was needed, she "wrote her essays to challenge feminists as well as misogynists of her era to examine their assumptions about equality" (Knepper 68).

In her essay "What Do Feminist Critics Want?" Sandra Gilbert outlines the philosophical basis for feminist criticism: "to decode and demystify all the disguised questions and answers that have always shadowed the connections between textuality and sexuality, genre and gender, psychosexual identity and cultural authority" (36). Surprisingly, many of these goals appear in the Harriet Vane novels, with Sayers always focusing, however, on the implications of these questions for humans of both sexes. Therefore, although it would be unwise to judge Sayers's work on the assumption that she, an educated, self-supporting woman, was a feminist, it is not unreasonable to expect her to work out her own humanistic scheme for equality among the sexes within her novels.

Evidence that many critics have not understood Dorothy L. Sayers's beliefs in forming their assumptions about her "feminist" platform becomes evident from their conception of Harriet as a model of feminist independence. Critical dismay at Harriet's "capitulation" to Lord Peter indicates that some feminist critics believed she had begun her life in Sayers's novels as an independent nontraditional woman, and had slowly changed, becoming more conventional over time. Disappointment with both Harriet and Sayers begins with a belief that the author is a feminist, and therefore her character should also be one. While I think the association with feminism is erroneous, this inclination to connect Sayers with her character is useful. As biographer Janet Hitchman put it, "there is no doubt that Harriet is Dorothy as she saw herself" (98). Biographer James Brabazon agrees: "[I]n her heroine, Harriet Vane, she was to paint a portrait of precisely the same problems [which Dorothy had]—a woman of distinction, intelligence, and strong clear emotions, but without conventional beauty" (72). Admitting that Sayers felt shackled to the Wimsey novels because of their financial success, he explains her use of Harriet in *Gaudy Night* and *Busman's Honeymoon*: "Here was a character who could express Dorothy's own vision of the world, whose thoughts could be Dorothy's thoughts, her perceptions Dorothy's perceptions, her emotions Dorothy's emotions" (148).

Sayers herself often spoke about an author's relationship with her characters, admitting the closeness, but carefully maintaining the creation's independence lest too much be revealed about the author. In *The Mind of the Maker* Sayers remarked that readers "do incline to suppose that a writer can be somehow cabined, cribbed, confined inside one of his 'favorite' characters . . . the reader is, of course, right this far: that a writer cannot create a character or express a thought or emotion which is not within his own mind" (51). I believe Sayers did use Harriet Vane as an outlet for many of her social concerns, which were decidedly not feminist in perspective; thus, we cannot expect her to create a feminist heroine. Like her creator, Harriet seems to have a broader concept of social revision, emphasizing the characteristics which all humans share.

Critics who do not like Harriet's marriage to Peter Wimsey do not see this more humanistic concern, or view it as a betrayal. They study Harriet's independent behavior in the first several novels and feel that her new relationship to Peter contradicts the self-sufficient lifestyle that Harriet seemed to possess. As Judge Crossley tells us in *Strong Poison*, Harriet was

left, at the age of twenty-three, to make her own way in the world. Since that time—she is now twenty-nine years old—she has worked industriously to keep herself, and it is very much to her credit that she has, by her own exertions, made herself independent in a legitimate way, owing nothing to anybody and accepting help from no one. (8)

Critics with dichotomous views of gender roles swiftly identify Harriet as feminist when they recognize the independence and professional success of this woman in the late 1920s. However, such a reading of Harriet Vane cannot grasp her actual situation. While Harriet is clearly industrious, successful, and self-sufficient, these things do not necessarily indicate *true, emotional* independence.

In the earlier novels, Harriet does not choose her independence, but has it forced on her by the traumas of her affair with Philip Boyes and her trial for his murder. Her personality and actions as they appear in the first three novels are not the norm for her, but represent abnormal behavior growing out of her recent experiences. Thus the supreme importance of *Strong Poison* in a study of this character, even though we see very little of Harriet in it. This novel introduces us to the trauma she went through with Boyes, and to the second, equal if not more terrific, trauma of the trial and public exposure of her affair. Thus, in *Strong Poison, Have His Carcase,* and most of *Gaudy Night*, Harriet is in a reactive state following these two horrible episodes and is necessarily inclined toward *isolation,* not actual independence. What some critics identify as a feminist encountering her world is actually a wounded, aggressively defensive, basically conservative woman fighting for her psychological and practical survival.

Before either trauma, Harriet acts in a most conventional, unfeminist way as she enters her affair with Boyes. Although the patriarchy views the relationship as unorthodox, the affair's structure mimics the typical marital relationship, with the female effacing herself to please her male partner. After her breakup with Boyes, Harriet becomes a social loner. The patriarchal judge at her trial interprets this as Harriet "refusing to thrust herself into company where her social outlawry might cause embarrassment" (*Strong Poison* 10). I would like to suggest that Harriet is not ashamed of her extramarital sexual affair, but of the step toward self-destruction she has taken in relinquishing her moral standards and accepting Boyes's as her own. Through isolation she has begun to prepare for the pain she knows must follow. Her drive for isolation is *reactive,* not chosen in quiet rationality. When Boyes's betrayal renders her utter devotion ridiculous, Harriet swings rapidly into an apparently independent—defensive—frame of mind, which is accentuated by the ensuing trial.

The growth of Harriet's apparent independence occurs because of continued traumatic circumstances, not because of feminist leanings. Harriet's imprisonment in *Strong Poison* is as much emotional as actual. Her emotional and physical isolation increased immediately upon Boyes's betrayal; still stinging from that "beastliness," she resolves to avoid similar encounters. Then, just as she begins to reenter society, the trial occurs and society actually plucks her from among itself and cordons her off. Suddenly Harriet finds the majority reviling her, condemning her sexual actions, and anxious to excise her. Unable to discover the interaction with others so important to regaining her self-esteem, Harriet retreats into an isolated defensive posture which begins to look, in *Have His Carcase,* like feminist independence.

Even in *Have His Carcase,* however, Harriet's independent actions seem forced upon her, not chosen, though she certainly does not complain and makes the best of the circumstances she encounters. Sayers opens the novel from Harriet's point of view, protesting against romantic involvement and highlighting the strengths of independence. "The best remedy for a bruised heart is not, as so many people seem to think, repose upon a manly bosom. Much more efficacious are honest work, physical activity, and the sudden acquisition of wealth" (7). Though already embarked on her solitary walking tour, Harriet feels it necessary to reassert to herself the advantages of independence. Harriet reminds herself that she will receive no forwarded letters, "and if she now and again gave a thought to Lord Peter Wimsey diligently ringing up an empty flat, it did not trouble her, or cause her to alter her steady course" (7). The thought doesn't trouble Harriet because, motivated by the trauma of Boyes's betrayal, she fears another relationship. Also, Harriet uses her walking tour to run away from herself and her inability to deal with her conflicting attitudes. Her romantic trauma has driven her to adopt a defensive independence and the social trauma has forced even more isolation upon her. But Peter Wimsey wants her to rejoin society, as his wife. While the man and the offer attract her, fears keep Harriet immobile, and the inner conflict slowly eats away at her nerves.

Even when the external circumstances of the murder of Paul Alexis direct her toward contact with Peter Wimsey, Harriet continues to resist, not out of a sense of feminist independence, but from fear sublimated through rationalization. This is made evident by her defiant over-justification of her reasons for steering clear of Peter. After she discovers the body of Paul Alexis and contacts the local police,

the image of Lord Peter kept intruding upon her mind . . . it would have been only fair to ring him up and tell him about the corpse with the cut throat. But under the circumstances, the action might be misinterpreted. And, in any case, the thing was probably only the dullest kind of suicide, not worth bringing to his attention. (42)

As discoverer of the body, Harriet knows full well Alexis's death did not result from "the dullest kind of suicide." This rationalization for not calling Peter indicates her emotional determination to keep her thoughts away from him.

As the third novel, *Gaudy Night,* begins, circumstances continue to force Harriet into isolation, whether she desires it or not. When Miss de Vine congratulates Harriet on her ability to express her beliefs frankly, the young woman indicates the conflict she feels within. " 'I disconcert myself very much. I never know what I do feel' " (41). Her continuing reaction to the trauma of Boyes's betrayal still separates her from Peter Wimsey and keeps her from achieving the kind of relationship she wants to have with him.

All Harriet's own tragedy had sprung from "persuading herself into appropriate feelings" towards a man whose own feelings had not stood up to the test of sincerity either. And all her subsequent instability of purpose had sprung from the determination that never again would she mistake the will to feel for the feeling itself. (42)

Even though she wants to feel, wants to enter into an intimate relationship with a man, she desperately needs to protect herself from a repetition of the earlier episode. Clearly Harriet is not simply a woman who disdains relationships with men as unnecessary to fulfillment in her life—she desires such a relationship but avoids it because of her emotional wounds.

Though the social trauma resulting from Harriet's trial for the murder of Boyes also continues to force independence upon her, Harriet makes great steps in regaining control over her life and reentering the social sphere when she decides to attend the gaudy—a formal gathering for students, alumnae, and professors. Schooled by the reactions she faced from other people during and following the trial, Harriet fears that her former teachers will not wish to see her; the social lesson she has so painfully learned over the last several years forces her to isolate herself. Settling in at the College, Harriet goes about her business "unspeaking and unspoken to, like a ghost" (11). This sense of isolation diminishes within the limited social sphere of Shrewsbury College as the weekend goes by and Harriet finds herself accepted by the members of the community. Her evident joy at being welcomed by the Dean, her old tutor, and the others without reference to her trial further supports the idea that Harriet's independence was more forced upon her than chosen. Harriet's continuing reactions to past traumas, not any feminist sense of prospering in an all female group, drives her to consider remaining within the Shrewsbury community. Spurned on moral grounds by the majority of the people in patriarchal society, Harriet yearns for the seclusion of this counter-culture, although her professional success depends upon her involvement in the world of London business.

These incidents from the first three Wimsey/Vane novels support the proposition that Harriet Vane was not a feminist at all, but that she appeared independent and isolated because she had been forced into such behavior by the events of her relationship with Boyes and her trial for his murder. Evaluation of Harriet's behavior in any of the novels must certainly consider her life prior to the events of *Strong Poison,* especially the stories of Harriet's childhood, and her interaction with Boyes. While many feminist critics attend to these issues, none have done so in consideration of Dorothy L. Sayers's heroine. These unwritten "novels" about Harriet are essential to understanding her behavior in the actual novels because they contain the history which motivates her present actions.

Examination of the little information Sayers gives us regarding Harriet Vane's childhood introduces the conflicting issues which seem to control her adulthood. Even though Sayers originally had no intention of continuing Peter or Harriet beyond *Strong Poison,* she later bases many of the issues implicit in that novel, as well as the following three novels, in this history. The developments of Harriet's childhood are Sayers's subsequent grounding of a humanistic ideal in Harriet's history, but the issues existed in the novels, and even in the author's history, prior to *Strong Poison*.

The issues at stake throughout the Wimsey/Vane novels and grounded in both Sayers's history and her character's, involve the concept of psychological androgyny, an idea essential to contemporary feminist thinking. Linda Olds explains that society generally views sex roles dichotomously. "Masculinity and femininity are conceptualized as polar opposites rather than qualities that can exist in different balances within each individual" (7). The concept of psychological androgyny involves "the relatively equal development within one person of the personality characteristics traditionally associated with men as well as women" (20). The archetypal masculine and feminine are mental rather than physical, states Barbara Greenfield (11). Thus an androgynous female, in addition to traditional female behaviors, would exhibit archetypal masculine behaviors "pertaining to activated spirit, intellect, and will" (11). Clearly, as Carolyn Heilbrun remarks, psychological androgyny "seeks to liberate the individual from the confines of the appropriate" (*Toward* x).

At the center of the androgynous development of a young woman lies her childhood relationship to her father. Discussing the development of both feminine and androgynous women, Olds notes that feminine women, as children, considered themselves "Daddy's little girl" (110), while androgynous women "tended to describe more intense relationships with their fathers, and sometimes thwarted attempts to be close and live up to their fathers' expectations" (111). Thus, the behaviors which androgynous women developed to "please their fathers were precisely those which would extend their repertoire beyond the traditional 'feminine' realm" (112). Heilbrun, in her afterword to a 1989 collection of essays studying fathers and daughters, remarked that biographies of successful androgynous women showed that their fathers propelled them beyond the normal woman's life in one of three ways: either 1) his disappointed desire for sons; 2) the example of his more "challenging, worldly, and exciting life compared with that of any woman within her sights"; or 3) his support of her intelligence and talents which encourages her to enter a world "in which she has no place" (419).

Biographic information on Dorothy L. Sayers suggests that she, from childhood, developed both masculine and feminine traits in her personality. "Her character unquestionably displays certain masculine elements. As a child she preferred beaten up toy monkeys to prettily dressed dolls . . . she also had an objective and analytical turn of mind" (Brabazon 16). Sayers herself remarked upon the androgynous pastimes of her childhood: "I dramatized myself . . . into a great number of egotistical impersonations of a very common type, making myself the heroine (or more often the hero) of countless dramatic situations" (qtd. in Brabazon 13). Here clearly is the activated spirit, intellect, and will of which Greenfield spoke.

Very little is known about Sayers's relationship to her father. Although Brabazon hints that Dorothy thought her mother the more intelligent of her parents (11), it seems clear that the young girl got support for androgynous inclinations from her father. Henry Sayers, a clergyman, had no sons, and though we have no evidence suggesting he felt disappointment that his only child was a daughter, certainly his active life as a clergyman appealed more to the inquisitive Dorothy than her mother's circle of spinster relatives. She could not have failed to observe that "to the villagers it was the rector who was the impressive figure," not her mother (Brabazon 11). Finally, Henry Sayers supported Dorothy's intellectual development, sending her to excellent schools and to Oxford even before women's degrees were granted. As Sayers matured, androgynous issues remained foremost in her social outlook. I have already discussed her concern for the improvement of the situations of both sexes and her emphasis on human similarities rather than gender differences. Previously I only pointed out that these attitudes differed fundamentally from feminism; now I want to stress that they express hopes for more androgynous freedoms.

Though we have little information about Harriet Vane's past life, what we do have suggests similarities between her childhood and Sayers's own, especially in the importance of the father's influence in the daughter's developing psychological androgyny. The only details we get about Harriet's parents match circumstances in Sayers's own childhood: both mothers are overshadowed by the fathers; both fathers are named Henry, and both do professional rounds, driving first a pony-trap and then an early model Ford (*Busman's Honeymoon* 50, Brabazon 10). Since these are the *only* details we receive about Harriet's parents, their significance is especially important.

In *Busman's Honeymoon*, Harriet's return to the neighborhood in which she grew up spurs on various memories; as she again meets local people from her childhood, one curious omission remains: neither Harriet herself nor any of the old acquaintances ever mentions her mother. Harriet's mother remains completely absent from her memories. Because mention of her father is relatively frequent in this novel, one must wonder if Harriet's mother died very early in her daughter's life, and thus did not live to inspire vivid memories. Or perhaps the woman is little remembered because she, like so many other women of the time, lived a life defining herself in terms of her husband, and never carved a niche or identity of her own. This latter suggestion seems supported by the only mention that such a person ever existed, Harriet's description of her parents to the Dowager Duchess: "quiet country doctor and wife" (32). Exactly what happened to her is of less importance than its effect on Harriet. Either her mother's actual physical absence or her lack of strong identity helped Harriet learn that women had less interesting existences than men.

The primary force in Harriet's young life is, without a doubt, her father, who exerts both positive and negative influences on his daughter's psychological development. Both of these influences are made clear through the picture we get of Harriet's relationship to her father as it appears in the single complete memory she has of him.

When she was quite small, Dr. Vane had had a dogcart—just like doctors in old fashioned books. She had gone along this road, ever so many times, sitting beside him, sometimes allowed to pretend to hold the reins. Later on, it had been a car—a small noisy one. . . . The doctor had had to start on his rounds in good time, so as to leave a margin for break-downs. The second car had been more reliable—a pre-war Ford. She had learnt to drive that one. (50)

Dr. Henry Vane's positive influence comes through his encouraging Harriet's androgynous development in the ways mentioned above. First, Dr. Vane had no sons. Harriet, like Dorothy Sayers, was her father's only child. Again, no evidence exists that he mourned the absence of a son, but the possibility exists and should not be ignored. Second, Dr. Vane encouraged Harriet's developing sense of professional independence by exposing her to the more interesting, active, vital life led by a man. Because Dr. Vane so frequently included Harriet on his rounds (an unusual circumstance perhaps necessitated by the absence of the mother), she learned early about the activities involved in a professional life and the satisfaction it could bring both to the professional and those he helped. When Harriet returns to her old home, locals praise his memory. Mrs. Ruddle admired him. "'I did 'ear as 'e'd passed away, and sorry I was—'e was a wonderful clever doctor, was your dad, miss—I 'ad 'im for my Bert, and I'm sure it's a mercy I did 'im comin' into the world wrong end up as you might say'" (56).

Finally, Dr. Vane encouraged the development of his daughter's talents and intellect throughout her young life. When she was a child he supported the imaginative adventures which would eventually earn her a living by allowing her to fantasize about being like her powerful father and holding the reins on the dogcart. This early imaginative experience leads to Harriet's movement toward independence when she actually learns to drive her father's pre-war Ford. Her thought, "she had learnt to drive *that* one" (my italics), seems to emphasize her triumph; even though she could only pretend to drive the first vehicle, she learned to do it for real later. I chose my emphasis because Sayers could easily have had Harriet remember that her father taught her to drive the second car, especially given the nostalgic nature of Harriet's musings. But this is not how Harriet remembers the events. She took the initiative, she reaped the success; she learned to control her father's machine and took her first step toward achieving independence and power. Dr. Vane also encouraged Harriet's intellectual abilities, always "very anxious . . . [that] H should have good education" (32), as the Dowager Duchess writes in her journal. Such an attitude would have been progressive in the early twentieth century, when university education for women was still a new idea. Clearly her father's encouragement taught Harriet pride in developing her intellectual faculties.

This evidence of the enlightened parenting Harriet received makes even more puzzling the tremendous problems she has with self-esteem and interpersonal relationships as an adult. Clearly this fathering was not so good that she could avoid troubles later; her independence was not developed enough that she could circumvent problems with dependence. While the absence of Harriet's mother contributed to this, what in Harriet's relationship to her father allowed this to happen?

Dr. Henry Vane's relationship to his daughter also contained some negative influences which undercut the androgynous lessons he taught her in more positive moments. The first of these was the lesson of the exclusivity of patriarchal power: things in life, including little girls, received value only by virtue of their relationship to the father. As Harriet reenters the world of her childhood in *Busman's Honeymoon*, she discovers that her memories of the villagers, and theirs of her, center on Dr. Vane. People unconnected to Dr. Vane are vague in her memory. Harriet only knows the local people who encountered the doctor. She knows very little about the Twittertons because "they weren't Dad's patients," even though they were neighbors in a small village. Likewise, the locals identified her as a child only in terms of her father, and continue to do so now. When the Reverend Goodacre becomes reacquainted with Harriet, he expresses delight, not with Harriet, but "at meeting Dr. Vane's daughter once more" (112). Young Harriet could hardly have avoided forming an impression of her father as supremely important, or learning that little girls got attention solely through their connections to men. Further suggestion that Harriet held an inflated perception of her father comes in her comparison of him to the fantasy characters in books: "Dr. Vane had had a dogcart—just like doctors in old fashioned books." We may see in this memory the beginnings of Harriet's later tendency to fantasize her men into elevated positions and archaic images, and thus subordinate herself to them, as manifested especially in her relationship with Philip Boyes.

The second negative lesson which Dr. Vane's behavior taught Harriet is opposite to the first: though powerful, patriarchs also suffer from a fundamental lack, and cannot be trusted to provide security and power consistently. This deficit appears with Henry Vane in two ways: his sudden, early death, and his financial failings. Implications that Harriet's father has failed her through his sudden, unexplained death surface in *Strong Poison* during Judge Crossley's summation. He tells us of Harriet, "who, through no fault of her own, was left, at the age of twenty-three, to make her own way in the world" (8). The judge's use of the terms "left" and "no fault of her own" make clear that, from his point of view, Harriet's situation was not her doing, and that someone else had performed inadequately in allowing it to happen. The words imply that she was abandoned, left to fend for herself with no relations and no legacy in a time when a young single woman would be hard put to support herself.

This lack of financial security constitutes the second paternal failure of which Dr. Henry Vane is guilty. Despite his commitment to Harriet's intellectual future, he seems curiously irresponsible in providing for her financially. The Dowager Duchess records in her diary Harriet's report that her "father made quite a good income" (*Busman's Honeymoon* 32); however, we learned in *Strong Poison* that upon his sudden death he had left no money at all behind him to help support his only child in a world not well suited to caring for young unmarried women. Having taught Harriet throughout her life that men, or at least he, could be counted on for financial security, Dr. Vane leaves her with nothing when he dies.

The overall message Harriet receives from her father's promotion of both androgyny and dependence is a complex, ambiguous one. Her father has taught her independence, but at the same time emphasized how much she needed him to achieve that "independence." Then as he taught her to depend upon paternal power, he left her without the power or the support she relied on, thus enforcing a lesson of independence. A confusing circle for a little girl and young woman to live through.

Perhaps the best indication of the way these ambiguous paternal messages influenced Harriet is her behavior immediately following her father's death. As Judge Crossley reminds us, Harriet supports herself not only successfully, but in such a way that she owes nothing to anybody and allows no one to aid her. Harriet fears to allow herself to depend on someone else to any extent for two reasons. First, such dependence necessarily involves a subordination of her own personality to the male's; and second, just when she begins to depend on the male totally, he leaves her psychologically and financially empty. This is precisely the pattern which emerges when Harriet does finally allow herself to depend on Philip Boyes. Harriet's only concept of male-female interaction developed through her relationship with her father; thus when she later becomes involved with Philip, she cannot help replicating that pattern, including the elements of it which she does not like. Because of the ambiguity of her father's message, Harriet, who has learned the ideal of androgyny, is not capable of implementing that idea in an adult relationship. Her awareness of androgyny renders most patriarchal men unattractive to her, but because of her lack of ego strength, Harriet requires a man who will provide the power and security she desires. Thus she looks for a man like her father and finds him in Philip Boyes: a man truly conventional and dominating—under the guise of unconventionality.

Though Harriet's relationship with Boyes turns out badly, it does help Harriet toward self-reliance. She does not again depend upon a male for financial security. *Strong Poison* is strewn with references to the miserable sales of Boyes's books and the financial success of Harriet's. So although Harriet still has much work to do reinterpreting her father's ambiguous lessons about emotional independence and dependence, she clearly has learned the importance of financial stability.

The story of the four Harriet Vane novels stems from these two unwritten narratives of Harriet's childhood and her relationship with Boyes. Without consideration of this background material a clear reading of her progress in the novels cannot be achieved. Harriet is not a feminist woman who slowly gives up her independence to marry an aristocrat; she has been from childhood a female with an androgynous ideal who feels she must maintain a contradictory dependence on a male to survive. Thus the novels are androgynous, not feminist. Heilbrun specifies the difference: "[I]n androgynous novels the reader identifies with the male and female characters equally; in a feminist novel, only with the female hero" (*Toward* 58). Certainly this is the case with the Wimsey/Vane novels; though I focus my own study primarily on Harriet Vane, much of the space in the novels, as in criticism, is devoted to Lord Peter.

This article has suggested where I think the fault lies with most feminist readings of Dorothy L. Sayers's heroine. In a curious and uncharacteristic omission, most female critics, usually so sensitive to psychological and biographical nuances, have not considered those in reading these novels. I believe Sayers in fact achieved precisely what many critics accuse her of abandoning: a series of novels which presents an ideal of independence and interaction for women. The series illustrates how Harriet's growth in the four novels moves her from an interpersonal self-definition in her relationship to Philip Boyes in *Strong Poison*, through a defensively motivated professional self-concept in *Have His Carcase* and *Gaudy Night* toward a reconciliation of her childhood traumas with her father and an understanding of her self in an androgynous context with Peter in *Busman's Honeymoon*.[4] Sayers has created in her Harriet Vane novels a travel narrative of the human psyche. While Harriet's apparent independence and tough-mindedness delight feminists, they are positive goals only in a culture, like our Western one, which values independence above all else. I think Sayers believed, as Robert Kegan later argued, that "highly differentiated psychological autonomy . . . may not be the fullest picture of maturity in the domain of the person" (228). It virtually ignores the other important human yearning, that for inclusion.

In these stories Sayers subverts this reigning myth of autonomy by attending to the underlying desire for inclusion. The Harriet Vane of *Have His Carcase* and *Gaudy Night* is not an example of self-sufficiency, and her marriage to Wimsey no abandonment of that ideal. Throughout the Vane novels, Sayers shows both human yearnings alive and struggling in Harriet, who finally achieves balance at the end of *Busman's Honeymoon*. Sayers shows Lord Peter Wimsey growing too; as he recognizes and accepts both yearnings within himself, he slowly helps Harriet to do the same. Far from letting other women down with the conclusion of her romance, Sayers has tried to lift up both women and men, carrying them beyond their cultural stagnation in interpersonal and institutional self-definitions and showing them the truth and integrity possible in the maturity of androgyny.

Notes

1. I encase "feminist" within quotation marks because the word can assume so many different meanings in critical discourse and in casual conversation. In this case, I mean anyone who calls herself "feminist" regardless of her definition of that term. Later in this article I will more clearly define the term, the ways critics use it, and the way in which Sayers herself employed the term.

2. Though the marriage of a female protagonist disappoints modern feminist critics, it was not unusual in its day. Recent studies of women's fiction of the late nineteenth and early twentieth centuries reveal a popular plot pattern which "presents the young woman's recognition of the superiority of marriage . . . over any form of feminine independence" (Gorsky 41). Heilbrun is not alone in her conclusion that "women writers do not imagine women characters with even the autonomy they themselves have achieved" (*Reinventing* 71).

3. Permission to quote from this letter, and all the others mentioned in this article, is not available. The letters can be reviewed at the Wade Center, Wheaton College, Wheaton, Illinois.

4. While length prevents me from an extended reading of *Busman's Honeymoon* here, critical inattention to that work also leaves me with little to discuss regarding women's reading of Sayers's development of her female protagonists. It seems worth mentioning, however, that marriage does not serve as a panacea for Harriet's anxieties. Ultimately, Sayers shows these can only be overcome if Harriet returns to the locale of her original troubles. There, through empathy, projection, and projective-identification, Harriet eventually faces and conquers her past, exorcising the ghosts which have prevented her from entering a truly androgynous relationship with Peter. The struggles she undergoes in this novel to achieve a marriage in which both partners are willing to assume and capable of assuming whichever role is required by their partner's needs are outlined in another of my papers: "Exorcising the Appropriate: Projection and Projective Identification in Dorothy L. Sayers' *Busman's Honeymoon." Studies in Psychoanalytic Theory* Oct. 1992.

Works Cited

Auerbach, Nina. *Romantic Imprisonment: Women and Other Glorified Outcasts*. New York: Columbia UP, 1985.

Brabazon, James. *Dorothy L. Sayers: A Biography*. New York: Avon, 1981.

Craig, Patricia, and Mary Cadogan. *The Lady Investigates: Women Detectives and Spies in Fiction*. New York: St. Martin's, 1981.

Gilbert, Sandra. "What Do Feminist Critics Want? A Postcard from the Volcano." *The New Feminist Criticism*. Ed. Elaine Showalter. New York: Pantheon, 1985. 29-45.

Gorsky, Susan. "The Gentle Doubters: Images of Women in Englishwomen's Novels, 1840-1920." *Images of Women in Fiction: Feminist Perspectives*. Ed. Susan Koppelman Cornillon. Bowling Green, OH: Bowling Green State University Popular Press, 1972. 28-54.

Greenfield, Barbara. "The Archetypal Masculine: Its Manifestation in Myth and Significance of Women." *The Father: Contemporary Jungian*

Perspectives. Ed. Andrew Samuels. Washington Square: New York UP, 1989. 187-210.

Heilbrun, Carolyn G. Afterword. *Daughters and Fathers.* Ed. Lynda E. Boose and Betty S. Flowers. Baltimore: Johns Hopkins UP, 1989. 418-23.

———. *Reinventing Womanhood.* New York: Norton, 1979.

———. *Toward a Recognition of Androgyny.* New York: Knopf, 1973.

Hitchman, Janet. *Such a Strange Lady.* London: New English Library, 1975.

Kegan, Robert. *The Evolving Self: Problem and Process in Human Development.* Cambridge: Harvard UP, 1982.

Klein, Kathleen Gregory. *The Woman Detective: Gender and Genre.* Urbana: U of Illinois P, 1988.

Knepper, Marty S. "Sexual Equality in Dorothy L. Sayers's Essays and her Peter Wimsey-Harriet Vane Novels." *Women and Equality: Selected Proceedings of the 1988 Women's Research Conference at the University of South Dakota.* Ed. Susan J. Wolfe, Jane D. Bromert, and Catherine A. Flum. Vermillion, SD: U of South Dakota, 1989. 58-72.

Olds, Linda E. *Fully Human: How Everyone Can Integrate the Benefits of Masculine and Feminine Sex Roles.* Englewood Cliffs, NJ: Prentice-Hall, 1981.

Peters, Margot, and Agate Nesaule Krouse. "Women and Crime: Sexism in Allingham, Sayers, and Christie." *Southwest Review* 59 (Spring 1974): 144-52.

Roller, Judi M. *The Politics of the Feminist Novel.* New York: Greenwood, 1988.

Sayers, Dorothy L. "Are Women Human?" *Unpopular Opinions.* London: Gollancz, 1946. 106-16.

———. *Busman's Honeymoon.* London: Gollancz, 1972.

———. *Gaudy Night.* London: Gollancz, 1972.

———. *Have His Carcase.* London: Gollancz, 1971.

———. "The Human-Not-Quite-Human." *Unpopular Opinions.* London: Gollancz, 1946. 116-22.

———. Letter to Miss Dorothy M.E. Dawson. 5 Aug. 1942. No. 158/56. Files in Marion E. Wade Center, Wheaton College.

———. Letter to Mrs. O.W. Campbell. 10 Sept. 1947. No. 158/26. Files in Marion E. Wade Center, Wheaton College.

———. *The Mind of the Maker.* New York: Harcourt, Brace, 1941.

———. *Strong Poison.* London: Gollancz, 1970.

Showalter, Elaine. "Toward a Feminist Poetics." *The New Feminist Criticism.* Ed. Elaine Showalter. New York: Pantheon, 1985. 125-43.

"E" Is for En/Gendering Readings:
Sue Grafton's Kinsey Millhone

Priscilla L. Walton

Sue Grafton launched her alphabetized detective series in 1982, with the publication of *"A" Is for Alibi*. The author of eleven Kinsey Millhone novels to date, she has produced approximately one book a year since 1982, each of which has enjoyed an enormous popularity. Grafton's success with mystery fiction is such that she is often hailed as an innovator of the Tough Gal Private Eye, and lauded as a re-vis(ion)er of crime writing. Her efforts (along with those of her "sisters in crime," Sara Paretsky and Marcia Muller) to open the conventionally sexist and exclusive hard-boiled detective mode to include women and women's issues have encouraged the production of a remarkable number of feminist detective novels. Since the bestselling status of Grafton's novels would indicate that her works are read by and appeal to women, I would like to explore the ways in which her writings serve to empower female readers and, hence, contribute to feminist discourse.[1]

Although there has been relatively little feminist scholarship devoted to the en/gendered nature of reading practices, that gender operates as a component in interpretative strategies is suggested by readers' responses to writers like Grafton. Indeed, assessments of feminist detective fiction will often vary according to the gender of the reader. As I have discovered through teaching these works and discussing them with students, friends, and colleagues, female readers often respond favorably to Grafton's Kinsey Millhone novels, where male readers frequently contest the success of her rewriting of hard-boiled male authors. Indeed, in one of the more perceptive articles on Grafton, "'Reader, I blew him away': Convention and Transgression in Sue Grafton," Peter J. Rabinowitz argues that Grafton's *"A" Is for Alibi* generates double readings which subvert the subversive content of the text. Rabinowitz finds that in this novel Kinsey Millhone can be "interpreted as a woman tamed and a woman punished. But however she oscillates, she never quite finds a new position in which to stand, and this transgressive novel suddenly finds itself springing back into the same familiar trajectories [of traditional hard-boiled detective fiction]"

101

(340). Ultimately, Rabinowitz suggests that Grafton's subversion and conformity run parallel in *"A" Is for Alibi,* and thus exemplify the ways in which a writer—and a character—can become imprisoned in genre. Rabinowitz's analysis of Grafton's novel is sympathetic and discerning, and its sophistication is perhaps most evident in the author's ability to acknowledge that readers of different backgrounds may interpret Grafton differently. Consequently, Rabinowitz concludes his essay by calling for a critique of his critique when he notes, it "would be interesting to see . . . whether readers who don't share my background as a white male academic apply similar or different strategies to the text" (340-41).

Rabinowitz's ability to position himself and his reading in relation to the female-authored text he examines opens a line of inquiry into an analysis of the ways in which subject positions influence reading strategies. The act of reading is a process which involves the development of an identificatory relationship between the protagonist and the reader. The ways in which one might identify with a character will vary according to one's position in relation to the world of the literary text and to the world at large. When a woman approaches novels like Grafton's, novels that play upon and undercut the sexist proclivities of the male detective "canon," her position as a woman is affirmed by the resistant text. When a male reader approaches the same text, he does not similarly experience the affirmative process. Although the split in en/gendered reader responses I have noted could be a coincidence, I think that it results from the differences in the cultural spaces that men and women occupy, spaces that influence readerly appreciation of feminist crime fiction—and, arguably, revisionary writings in general.

I would suggest that the diverse and en/gendered responses to Grafton derive from the discrepancy in men's and women's cultural locations. Woman's experience of the world diverges from that of man since her relationship with the world is established on a different basis. I want to stress, before proceeding, that I am not suggesting that all women (or men) read in the same way and hence that all women (or men) *are* the same; but, rather, I wish to argue that women occupy a cultural site that allows for a generalized explication of woman's experience of the world. I want to draw on Teresa de Lauretis's explication of experience to elucidate my position. De Lauretis explains:

by experience, I do not mean the mere registering of sensory data, or a purely mental (psychological) relation to objects and events, or the acquisition of skills and competences by accumulation or repeated exposure. I use the term not in the individualistic, idiosyncratic sense of something belonging to one and exclusively her own even though others might have "similar" experiences; but rather in the general sense of a process by which, for all social beings, subjectivity is constructed. Through that process one places oneself or is placed in social reality, and so perceives and comprehends as subjective (referring to, even originating in, oneself) those relations—material, economic, and interpersonal—which are in fact social and, in a larger perspective, historical. The process is continuous, its achievement unending or daily renewed. For each person, therefore, subjectivity is an ongoing construction, not a fixed point of departure or arrival from which one then interacts with the world. On the contrary, it is the effect of that interaction which I call experience; and thus it is produced not by external ideals, values, or material causes, but by one's personal, subjective, engagement in the practices, discourses, and institutions that lend significance (value, meaning, and affect) to the events of the world. (159)

De Lauretis's suggestion that experience derives from social location allows for a theoretical discussion of the ways in which the differences in cultural placement of men and women will generate different reading strategies.

Historically, where man has operated as a subject of discourse, woman has been posited as the object of discourse and, thus, constructed as a passive receiver rather than an active performer. As feminist psychoanalytic critics argue, the feminine "I" has functioned in mimicry of the masculine "I" because patriarchy has not accorded woman a position from which to speak. When woman does assume a subject position, therefore, or tries to perform as the "I" of the discourse, the "I" she adopts is displaced and deferred (Grosz 72). Her "I" serves as a shadow of his "I," or becomes a transformed "you" in relation to him; she does not—because she cannot—speak as "author," since she has no author-ity. What this means, in practical terms, is that women have been discursively conditioned to accept a subordinate position, a position that is reinforced through their consistent social disenfranchisement.

This disenfranchisement of female subjectivity has a direct bearing on interpretative strategies. As Laura Mulvey in her 1975 article "Visual Pleasure and Narrative Cinema" argued in relation to film, the position of the viewer is traditionally encoded as male; woman is figured through her "to-be-looked-at-ness," rather than as the looker (436). Mulvey's argument points to the ways in which woman has been forced to assume the viewing position of man in order to participate as a viewer of film. No space has been accorded to her as subject, and, consequently, she cannot view "as a woman," since she cannot identify—as a subject—with women on the screen. She watches these cinematic women being watched, a situation that reinforces her own objectification. The process of reading a book is similar to "reading" a film in that female subjectivity remains a contested space in conventional fiction. Grafton and writers like her, I would argue, inscribe a subject position for women, and this inscription allows for female readers to read "as women." Femininity is affirmed in these texts, not derided or elided.

I suspect that the en/gendered responses I have noticed in relation to feminist crime writing result from woman's affirmation in and through these novels. That is, when a female reader is confronted with a female writer's effort to counter and subvert the "canonical" conventions of hard-boiled (male) detective fiction, she does not generally read in an effort to subvert the subversion. For her to read Grafton "against the grain," as does Rabinowitz, would be to undercut herself. Because she has a political stake in accepting the work—her subject position is validated within it—she responds differently from her male counterpart. A man, who has not been cast, consistently, as the object of discourse, might well miss the political ramifications of the inscribed female subjectivity, since it does not diverge from what he has been conditioned to expect for himself. A woman, whether consciously or unconsciously, responds to the female subjectivity that is established in the texts and reinforced through her reading of them.

I want to turn, now, to Grafton to examine the ways in which female subjectivity is implemented in her novels. Kinsey Millhone speaks the "I" of the first-person narration of Grafton's novels, and while this alone would not designate a shift from the expected female "you" to a female "I"/eye (in traditional texts, female characters often simulate a first-person narrative voice, but this does not indicate their exhibition of subjectivity),[2] her "I" carries with it a subjective authority that is lacking in more conventional works. Kinsey's "I"/eye is supported through the narrative content, which advocates an authoritative feminine subjectivity. Throughout Grafton's series, Kinsey indulges in generalizations that work to affirm the subjectivity of herself and her female readers. For instance, when Kinsey deliberately switches common gender pronoun assumptions, her strategy draws attention to the culturally conditioned expectation that woman will occupy a place subordinate to man's. In *"J" Is for Judgment,* Kinsey confides: "Every case is different, and every investigator ends up flying by the seat of her (or his) pants" (119). The switch from the expected "his pants," or the more common contemporary version, "his (or her) pants," repositions woman and "her" pants as the subject of the sentence; "she" does not function as an occlusion or an afterthought. There is a conscious effort here to establish woman as a primary subject, and this effort is borne out in the ways in which women and women's traditional activities are recuperated and validated in the novels.

Historically, women in the West have been relegated to the home and then taught to view their occupation as inconsequential and meaningless. Grafton's novels reposition domestic duties as valuable learned skills. Kinsey is not a domesticated or conventional woman, but her references to domestic activities authorize the value of woman's traditional space. In *"B" Is for Burglar,* Kinsey moves to recuperate the worth of woman's domestic training: "I was going to have to check it out item by item. I felt as if I were on an assembly line, inspecting reality with a jeweller's loupe. There's no place in a P.I.'s life for impatience, faintheartedness, or sloppiness. I understand the same qualifications apply for housewives" (33). Through passages like this, Grafton's novels perform an important function in affirming women who have been taught to trivialize and debase the abilities they have cultivated in their domestication.[3]

Where the de-valuation of domestic skills is common parlance in patriarchal discourse, Grafton's generous use of domestic analogies serves to substantiate the importance of the duties women have performed in the home. Indeed, the home is posited as a sort of base training camp for coping with the professional world, and the novels demonstrate how woman's domestication has better equipped her to act in the professional world. Often, Kinsey will equate the inner domestic sphere with the outer professional sphere. As she recounts in *"A" Is for Alibi*:

I did a couple of personal errands and then went home. It had not been a very satisfying day but then most of my days are the same: checking and cross-checking, filling in blanks, detail work that was absolutely essential to the job but scarcely dramatic stuff. The basic characteristics of any good investigator are a plodding nature and infinite patience. Society has inadvertently been grooming women to this end for years. (27)

This comparison serves to close the patriarchally constructed gap that separates the inner and the outer worlds. Those two spheres are bridged here, and the bridge foregrounds their interdependence—it does not downgrade one at the expense of the other.

Kinsey often contrasts herself with her male colleagues (within novels and media), and highlights the differences apparent in their work on a case. In *"F" Is for Fugitive,* the P.I. compares the ways in which she operates to the ways in which a male P.I. would function. She bemoans: "I felt like I'd spent half my time on this case washing dirty dishes. How come Magnum, P.I., never had to do stuff like this?" (159). Just as woman has been constructed as an "expert" in the kitchen, so she has been taught that she is helpless outside of it. In *"J" Is for Judgment,* Kinsey reiterates the patriarchally held view that women are unable to master technical concepts, and highlights the sexism that underpins such perceptions of men's and women's traditional activities: "Boys know about these things: guns, cars, lawn mowers, garbage disposals, electric switches, baseball statistics. I'm scared to take the lid off the toilet tank because that ball thing always looks like it's on the verge of exploding" (206). By juxtaposing the expectations placed on men and on women, Grafton is able to foreground the masculinist construction of those expectations. Where, in the earlier passage, Magnum is not required to wash dishes, women have not been required to learn the "mechanical" skills denoted in the above quotation. The difference between the two constructions, of course, is patriarchally loaded: Magnum does not have to do dishes because it is beneath him (and, presumably, because he can rely on some woman to do them for him), but women do not exhibit technical prowess because it is beyond their comprehension.

Despite her valorization of feminine capabilities, however, Kinsey does acknowledge how little women's skills are valued in the patriarchal world. The inequity of salaries, therefore, becomes an issue in *"I" Is for Innocent,* when Kinsey discovers that the (male) P.I. on the case before her charged $50 an hour. She comments, wryly, "Morley was getting fifty? I couldn't believe it. Either men are outrageous or women are fools. Guess which, I thought. My standard fee has always been thirty bucks an hour plus mileage" (23). While this passage suggests that women are foolish in underestimating their abilities, it also serves as a reminder that women have been conditioned to regard their abilities as second-rate and, thus, taught to participate in their own disempowerment.

Kinsey refuses to re-imprison woman in a sexist fashion by trivializing her domesticity, and rather attacks the areas where woman is patriarchally constricted. Clothing, which women have been conditioned to value, is devalued in Grafton's texts. Kinsey herself wears jeans and turtleneck sweaters, and has, for more formal occasions, an "all-purpose black dress" which is: "black with long sleeves, in some exotic blend of polyester you could bury for a year without generating a crease" (*"I"* 216). Traditional feminine footwear is disparaged when Kinsey notes that she has never been able to wear high heels: "I have friends who adore high heels, but I can't see the point. I figure if high heels were so wonderful, men would be wearing them" (*"I"* 216). Where that which has been forced upon women (and then used to trivialize them) is ridiculed, however, articles of clothing which are unmentionable/s in patriarchal discourse—as well as the object of much male humor—are not only mentioned, but are constructed as multipurpose garments. Kinsey's references to feminine underclothing—and their bizarre usages—provide for comic relief in several of Grafton's texts. Trapped in a hotel room, in *"G" Is for Gumshoe,* listening to the lovemaking of her neighbors through the wall, Kinsey acts as follows: "[I] stuffed a sock in each cup of my bra and tied it across my head like earmuffs, with the ends knotted under my chin. Didn't help much. I lay there, a cone over each ear like an alien, wondering at the peculiarities of human sex practices. I would have much to report when I returned to my planet" (87). This move to recuperate an aspect of femininity that has been derided serves as a means of reappropriating the trappings of femininity and re-positing them in a favorable light.

Perhaps most importantly, throughout her novels Grafton works to assert the value of femininity. In an age where the single white female has been vilified as the target of a backlash against women, in general, and feminists, in particular, as Susan Faludi so aptly argues in *Backlash: The Undeclared War against American Women,* Kinsey's delight in her single state serves to endorse the status of growing numbers of single women. In *"D" Is for Deadbeat,* Kinsey notes: "I love being single. It's almost like being rich" (21). In addition, Kinsey makes it clear that she *likes* women and takes pleasure in the appearance of women's bodies. *"C" Is for Corpse* provides a meaningful example of the ways in which Grafton repositions the female body, a body that has been the object of scrutiny by men from time immemorial. Rather than objectifying women, Kinsey watches women in a women's locker room and comments approvingly on their shapes and sizes: "women paraded back and forth in various stages of undress. It was a comforting sight. So many versions of the female breast, of buttocks and bellies and pubic nests, endless repetitions of the same forms. These women seemed to feel good about themselves and there was a camaraderie among them that I enjoyed" (108). This is an important passage, particularly in light of the ways in which women have tried and continue to try to live up to male standards of female beauty, a situation that has led to an epidemic of anorexia and bulimia as well as to a rise in self-destructive "beautification" measures—like liposuction and plastic surgery. There are no impossible standards of feminine beauty outlined here; indeed, there are no "standards" set at all. Kinsey simply enjoys the look of femininity—whatever shape or size it happens to assume.

Grafton not only takes pains to critique male standards of feminine beauty, she also works to delineate positive interaction between women and, hence, to undermine the sexist notion that women perceive each other as competitors for men. Rejecting the position of the envious woman, Kinsey takes delight in her best friend's attractiveness. Woman's appearance is also re-visioned through an undercutting of the patriarchal truism that "men don't make passes at women who wear glasses," since Kinsey's friend, Vera, sports glasses with "tortoiseshell rims and big round lenses tinted the color of iced tea. She wore glasses so well it made other women wish their eyesight would fail" (*"B"* 64).

Constructive portrayals of women, in whatever walk of life, abound in the Kinsey Millhone novels. What is perhaps most striking here is that Kinsey frequently crosses class boundaries and shows a marked appreciation of women working in traditionally marginalized spheres. In *"A" Is for Alibi*, Kinsey engages in conversation with Ruth, the secretary in a law office. This passage invokes the strength of female bonding, and also subverts expectations of "feather-brained" secretaries. Kinsey appraises Ruth's abilities and comments on the skills involved in secretarial work (reminiscent of her positive re-evaluation of housewifery):

Her husband had left her for a younger woman (fifty-five) and Ruth, on her own for the first time in years, had despaired of ever finding a job, as she was then sixty-two years old, "though in perfect health," she said. She was quick, capable, and of course was being aced out at every turn by women one-third her age who were cute instead of competent.

"The only cleavage I got left, I sit on," she said and then hooted at herself. (23)

Ruth's story also highlights the plight of middle-aged women who have been cast on the rag heap because their aging appearance supposedly renders them useless. Kinsey's assessment of the aging Ruth's usefulness, therefore, provides a significant commentary on the patriarchal belief that when women can no longer bear children, their purpose in life is over.

In *"C" Is for Corpse*, the "aging" woman makes another appearance and this time provides Kinsey with the opportunity to contrast the changes that have taken place in women's acceptance of other women. In this case, Lila, the older woman Kinsey encounters, has unquestioningly accepted her patriarchal training and perceives other women as threats. Kinsey notes: "I like older women as a rule. I like almost all women, as a matter of fact. I find them open and confiding by nature, amusingly candid when it comes to talk of men. This one was of the old school: giddy and flirtatious. She'd despised me on sight" (13-14). In this novel, Lila is attempting to bilk Kinsey's neighbor, Henry, of his life savings, and it is interesting that it is the older woman's distrust of women that renders her suspect. Women who like women are appraised favorably.

Kinsey never takes gratuitous pleasure in demeaning women or condemning lifestyles different from her own. In *"E" Is for Evidence,* she reflects on the lifestyle of the wealthy—and traditional—Olive Kohler, and acknowledges: "I'd begun to feel very charitable about Olive, whose life-style only yesterday had seemed superficial and self-indulgent. Who was I to judge? It was none of my business how she made her peace with the world. She'd fashioned a life out of tennis and shopping, but she managed to do occasional charity work, which was more than I could claim" (110). While Kinsey may learn to appreciate Olive's position, however, that position is undermined in the text. Killed by the husband who wishes to possess her, Olive figures the dangers of leading a patriarchally inscribed life. Olive's choice of lifestyle is dignified by Kinsey, but it is nonetheless dramatized in the novel as a risky, if not fatal, undertaking and contrasted with the more fruitful possibilities envisioned through feminine independence.

Perhaps one of Kinsey's most appealing characteristics is her fiercely independent nature. Glenwood Irons, in his essay, "New Women Detectives: G is for Gender-Bending," perceives Grafton as less feminist than Sara Paretsky because her novels conform to the ethos of American individualism:

If Grafton has created a feminist detective, it is to the extent that Kinsey Millhone fulfils Marty Knepper's definition of feminists as "women capable of intelligence, moral responsibility, competence and independent action . . . [who reject] sexist stereotypes." Unlike Paretsky's V.I. Warshawski, Kinsey is not interested in the power of female bonding, rather, she has "engendered" the macho tough-guy detective with a woman's perspective, a project quite different from the strength-from-bonding created by Paretsky. (135)

While I do not, by any means, wish to deride the radical undercutting of sexist hard-boiled detective fiction I believe Paretsky's writings to manifest,[4] I also believe that Irons's argument points up the problems of assuming that what is problematic in the hands of white male writers carries the same negative overtones when transcribed in the hands of women or members of minority groups. Cultural placement must be taken into consideration, here, in that feminine independence has repercussions different from those of male individualism.

Kinsey's assumption of a loner status is not the same as an imposition of masculine selfhood, a subtlety that is emphasized in Grafton's novels through Kinsey's carefully constructed autonomy. Not surprisingly, Kinsey's independence is dearly bought, and comprises her defensive stance against a patriarchal world which seeks to subordinate her. In keeping with the problematics of heterosexual relationships, feminine in/dependence becomes a troublesome strand in *"G" Is for Gumshoe,* when Kinsey falls in love with her hired bodyguard, Robert Dietz. Like many women, Kinsey becomes dependent on Dietz, and her dependence is particularly disturbing because Grafton has taken such pains, throughout the series, to maintain the self-sufficiency of her protagonist. Indeed, as the following passage indicates, Kinsey begins to bow to Dietz's "superior" judgment:

On our way to the firing range, we stopped by the gun shop and spent an hour bickering about guns. He knew far more than I did and I had to yield to his expertise. I left a deposit on an H&K P7 in 9-millimeter, filling out all the necessary paperwork. I ended up paying twenty-five bucks for fifty rounds of the Winchester Silvertips Dietz had insisted on. In exchange for my compliance, he had the good taste not to mention that all of this was his idea. I'd expected to find it galling to take his advice, but in reality, it felt fine. What did I have to prove? He'd been at it a lot longer than I had and he seemed to know what he was talking about. (185)

Kinsey's submission to Dietz's judgment does not go unmarked in the text, however. Cleverly, Grafton contrasts Kinsey's dependence on Dietz with that of Irene Gersh's dependence on her husband, in the textual subplot. Irene is dependent to the point where she is helpless without the guidance of others and is immobilized by the prospect of filling out her mother's death certificate by herself:

She seemed to collect herself. She nodded mutely, eyes fixed on me with gratitude as I moved into the adjacent room. I gathered up a pen and the eight-by-eight-inch square form from the desk and returned to the couch, wondering how Clyde endured her dependency. Whatever compassion I felt was being overshadowed by the sense that I was shouldering a nearly impossible burden. (233)

Grafton contrasts the two forms of dependence in this novel and problematizes both. Where the independent Kinsey comes close to surrendering her selfhood to Dietz, Irene's loss of selfhood constitutes a trap for dismissive readers. Irene is dependent because she has been traumatized as a child, a trauma that has gone undiscovered—and even led to her construction by the male medical establishment as an untreatable hysteric—until Kinsey begins to investigate a twenty-year-old murder. Kinsey unearths the reasons behind Irene's fears, reasons that presumably will enable Irene to function more purposefully, but the P.I. seems unable to save herself from the dependent relationship she has developed with Dietz. Dietz leaves for Germany at the end of the novel, thereby removing the threat of dependency from Kinsey, and their interaction highlights the difficulties resulting from the intricate power balances always at play in heterosexual relationships.

Irons's failure to distinguish the political difference between male and female independence is a miscalculation to which many critics fall prey. The shift in subject positioning must be taken into consideration when readers and critics approach Grafton, or the subversion and affirmation embodied in her fiction will get lost. Ward Churchill, for example, perceives the recent innovations in detective fiction (feminist and Other-wise) as ideological justifications for a repressive social system. In relation to Grafton, specifically, Churchill charges that: "Sue Grafton's Kinsey Millhone . . . is more of a 'tried-and-true grand-daughter of Marlowe and Spade,' demonstrating that in the new American sensibility, it's sometimes okay for women (but never men) to comport themselves like macho thugs" (285). Churchill's appraisal of Kinsey as a "macho thug" may seem rather harsh to (female) readers who have taken pleasure in the alternatives they find her to offer to "canonical" hard-boiled detectives like Sam Spade and Philip Marlowe, but if the divergent cultural sites the detectives occupy are ignored, the differences in their political positions are rendered inconsequential. Since Kinsey does not operate in a literary vacuum, her actions are more appropriately viewed as a re-action, for she is performing in response to her sexist forefathers.

Where Churchill, like Irons, does not place Grafton in a cultural and historical context, other critics do, and yet find her novels troublesome. Disturbingly, Grafton has been criticized by female critics who contend that her texts violate feminist principles. Kathleen Gregory Klein argues that female characters who validate traditional social structures demonstrate

the primacy of the conventional private-eye fictional formula over the feminist ideology which falsely seems to signal a change in the genre. Ironically, Grafton, McCone, and Steiner's novels demonstrate a triumph of the genre over feminist ideology in much the same way that patriarchal/sexist ideology triumphs over the genre in most of the preceding novels. (221)

Klein offers an important critique of Grafton, and she astutely points out the uneasy relationship that exists between the author and her feminist sympathies. On a textual level, the killers in the Kinsey Millhone novels are as often female as male (six of the eleven novels depict female murderers), and as a result, the texts work to reinforce a stereotype of murderous women that has no basis in statistical reality.

In addition, the ideological impetus of the novels wavers, perhaps reflecting Grafton's own discomfort with feminism. In a 1989 interview with Bruce Taylor, published as "G is for (Sue) Grafton," the author confided, "I am a feminist from way back" (11); but she retracts her statement in a 1992 interview with Daniel Richler for the TVOntario program *Imprint* and contends:

To me, writing is not about gender. And to me to imply that women are in any way at a disadvantage seems incorrect. . . . I don't see women as victims. I don't see women as one down. I don't believe we need to herd together in order to have power in the world. So what I prefer to do is to operate out of my own system, wherein, in some ways, I think I'm doing just as much for women by being out on the front lines by myself.

Grafton's inconsistent adherence to feminist politics when interviewed is distressing, and even convenient in light of the current backlash against women. (Her statement also provides a marked contrast to Paretsky's response to the same question: "You know, any more, when people ask me if I'm a feminist, I'm sort of tempted to say: 'Call me a strident bitch and smile when you say it'" [*Imprint* interview]). But, as a friend and colleague pointed out to me, to dismiss Grafton as a result of her statements is also convenient, since it is to hold the author to account for the situation that has presumably led her to retract her feminist sympathies. In that Grafton is a writer in the public eye, who must publish novels in order to support herself, her position must be placed in the context of bestselling fiction, which depends upon a large and diverse audience. Before one condemns a female writer for her political stance, that writer's position as a working woman should be figured into the assessment, since her statements may derive from her fear of alienating a wide audience.[5]

I also think that the politics of formula fiction should be weighed when evaluating the success or failure of the subversion of genre conventions in feminist crime writing. As John G. Cawelti has noted, formula fiction, in particular, depends upon well-established conventional structures that contribute to its formulation and "reflect the interests of audiences, creators, and distributors" (124). Mass-market fiction relies upon its formula to generate readership. It therefore cannot subvert generic conventions to such an extent that it becomes unrecognizable to readers of the formula, since to do so would be to estrange the audience on which the fiction depends. And, when Cawelti draws attention to endemic characteristics of formula fiction, he also, by extension, illuminates an aspect of Grafton's writing that is particularly important. Cawelti argues that formula fiction has the ability to assist in the process of assimilating changes in cultural values. He observes, in relation to westerns:

The western has undergone almost a reversal in values over the past fifty years with respect to the representation of Indians and pioneers, but much of the basic structure of the formula and its imaginative vision of the meaning of the West has remained substantially unchanged. By their capacity to assimilate new meanings like this, literary formulas ease the transition between old and new ways of expressing things and thus contribute to cultural continuity. (143)

Grafton, as the author of formula novels, who writes within a rigidly delineated genre, is—at least to a certain extent—necessarily caught within the problematics of her narrative form. But, given the cultural anxiety that feminism has generated in the last twenty years, the writings of Grafton (and female authors like her), provide a venue for assimilating some of the cultural changes that have taken place. It therefore need not follow that Grafton's adherence to the genre conventions of hard-boiled fiction renders her writings supportive of patriarchal constructions, or mars their contribution to feminist practice. I would argue that Grafton's texts enable readers, and female readers in particular, to explore the dynamics of gender constructions. Indeed, Grafton's fiction may well be extremely reflexive of woman's concerns precisely because they embody a compromise. Mimetically, the novels mirror woman's position in the world, for they deal with the world constructed through the hard-boiled mode and work to feminize it. Grafton's fiction does not attempt to create a new textual world, but rather deals with the problems inherent in the one with which her character is faced. The end result is of course a compromise—but, then, is not feminist practice, itself, always/already a compromise?

Grafton's novels do offer affirmation to the women to whom they are addressed. Hence, while the author may not radically subvert the detective formula, and while her politics may be problematic, she nonetheless works to implement female subjectivity in and through her writings, and affords women an opportunity to experience the assumption of a subject position. These aspects of Grafton's writings constitute a profound achievement, and when they are linked with positive depictions of woman's traditional roles, and with a character who actually *likes* other women, the end result manifests a powerful valorization of femininity. This woman writer's woman detective provides her women readers with a refreshing change from conventional depictions of femininity. And such a change is not only important to the world of detective fiction, in particular, it is also crucial to feminist movement in general.

Notes

1. Many of the ideas developed in this essay have arisen out of discussions with Manina Jones in relation to our book-in-progress, "Detective Agency: Women Re-Writing the Hardboiled Tradition." I am also indebted to Jamie Barlowe for her invaluable input into this article.

2. *The Turn of the Screw* provides an excellent example of the ways in which a female character may attempt to assume a subject position, but is disenfranchised within the narrative. See my essay "'What then on earth was I?': Feminine Subjectivity and *The Turn of the Screw*," in *Case Studies in Contemporary Criticism: The Turn of the Screw*, Bedford Books, 1994.

3. Grafton's texts inscribe a generalized white middle-class reader. This is not to suggest that they cannot be read by women outside of that cultural site, but rather that the values and the lifestyle they reflect are predominantly white and middle-class. Kinsey is a working woman, with pretensions to lower-class sensibilities, but her lifestyle is firmly in line with middle-class conventions.

It should also be noted that Grafton's treatment of race is disturbing. There are few women of color in her novels, and those characters belonging to minority groups—particularly those of Hispanic background—are depicted in a condescending fashion that veers on the judgmental. In *"H" Is for Homicide*, for example, Grafton posits a particularly troublesome view of Mexican-American culture. Ultimately, the "success" of the novel lies in the recuperation of Bibianna Diaz into a white middle-class superstructure through her alliance with a white police officer, an alliance that involves her rejection of the "criminal" element embodied in men of her own culture.

4. See my article, "Paretsky's V.I. as P.I.: Revising the Script and Recasting the Dick," in *Literature/Interpretative/Theory* 4 (1993): 203-13.

5. My thanks to Neal Ferris for this insight.

Works Cited

Cawelti, John G. "The Study of Literary Formulas." *Detective Fiction: A Collection of Critical Essays.* Ed. Robin W. Winks. Englewood Cliffs: Prentice-Hall Inc., 1980. 121-43.

Churchill, Ward. *Fantasies of the Master Race.* Ed. M. Annette Jaimes. Monroe, ME: Common Courage, 1992.

De Lauretis, Teresa. *Alice Doesn't: Feminism, Semiotics, Cinema.* Bloomington: Indiana UP, 1984.

Grafton, Sue. *"A" Is for Alibi.* New York: Bantam, 1987.

—. *"B" Is for Burglar.* New York: Bantam, 1986.

—. *"C" Is for Corpse.* New York: Bantam, 1987.

—. *"D" Is for Deadbeat.* New York: Bantam, 1988.

—. *"E" Is for Evidence.* New York: Bantam, 1989.

—. *"F" Is for Fugitive.* New York: Bantam, 1990.

—. *"G" Is for Gumshoe.* New York: Fawcett Crest, 1990.

—. *"H" Is for Homicide.* New York: Fawcett Crest, 1991.

—. *"I" Is for Innocent.* New York: Henry Holt, 1992.

—. *"J" Is for Judgment.* New York: Henry Holt, 1993.

—. *"K" Is for Killer.* New York: Henry Holt, 1994.

Grosz, Elizabeth. *Jacques Lacan: A Feminist Introduction.* London: Routledge, 1990.

Irons, Glenwood. "New Women Detectives: G Is for Gender-Bending." *Gender, Language, and Myth: Essays on Popular Narrative.* Ed. Glenwood Irons. Toronto: U of Toronto P, 1992.

Klein, Kathleen Gregory. *The Woman Detective: Gender and Genre.* Urbana: U of Illinois P, 1988.

Mulvey, Laura. "Visual Pleasure and Narrative Cinema." *Feminisms: An Anthology of Literary Theory and Criticism.* Ed. Robyn R. Warhol and Diane Price Herndl. New Brunswick: Rutgers UP, 1991. 432-42.

Rabinowitz, Peter J. " 'Reader, I Blew Him Away': Convention and Transgression in Sue Grafton." *Famous Last Words: Changes in Gender & Narrative Closure.* Ed. Alison Booth. Charlottesville: U of Virginia P, 1993. 326-46.

Richler, Daniel. "Interview." *Imprint.* Toronto: TVOntario, 1992.

Taylor, Bruce. "G is for (Sue) Grafton: An Interview with the Creator of the Kinsey Millhone Private Eye Series Who Delights Mystery Fans as She Writes Her Way Through the Alphabet." *Armchair Detective* 22.1 (1989): 4-13.

D.R. Meredith's Lydia Fairchild:
Frustrated Feminist

Paula M. Woods

Touted on book covers as the John Lloyd Branson series, D.R. Meredith's *Murder By* . . . novels, set in the Texas Panhandle, feature not only Branson but also his law clerk, Lydia Fairchild. Over the course of the first five novels of the series, Lydia Fairchild is a developing character against whom John Lloyd Branson also develops. Their relationship is a study in Freudianism as Meredith shows how Lydia tries to assert her independence from Branson the father, seeming to succeed gradually in the first four novels but retreating in the fifth.

When asked if she had modeled Fairchild on anyone, Meredith replied that the inspiration had come from several high school girls who had worked in her bookstore. She was intrigued by how different they were from women of her generation at the same age. These young women, she said, like Lydia, considered themselves the equal of any man, but they were not feminist men bashers—they had gone "beyond that."[1] Judging from these remarks, Meredith would not consider herself a feminist, but she has created a female character who does think of herself as a feminist.[2]

Meredith establishes a strong element of the formulaic romance novel in the series. In *Murder by Impulse*, the first book, Lydia is supposed to enjoy reading romances, so the conflict between the young, beautiful, rather naive woman and older, experienced, handsome, dangerous man can be seen as appropriate for her personality. Branson brings up her reading habits again in *Murder by Masquerade* by reminding her, "Innocent young ladies in your romance novels don't fall over dead bodies, Lydia" (182). And in *Murder by Sacrilege* when she remarks that she feels like a governess in a pornographic novel, Branson again teases her about her reading habits. The romance formula is interjected into the mystery conventions. There is the usual sparring between the two. By the end of the fourth novel, *Murder by Reference*, the romance is still simmering and Fairchild is beginning to demonstrate a degree of independence from Branson. But at the end of *Sacrilege,* the fifth novel, their romance is no longer simmering but at a full rolling

117

boil—typical of the romance novel, even if it has taken them longer than usual. It is, after all, a series.

Inherent in the romance relationship is a parody of the father-daughter relationship dear to Freudian critics. Fairchild's chafing under Branson's tutelage fairly reeks of penis envy. As Chodorow explains in *The Reproduction of Mothering*, girls, according to Freud "turn to their father, who has a penis and might provide them with this much desired appendage. . . . Finally they change from wanting a penis from their father to wanting a child from him, through an unconscious symbolic equation of penis and child" (94). Lydia lacks and desires not the physical phallus but knowledge and experience in detection and the law, the "social privileges of the father and men" symbolized by the penis (164-65). The phallus is a symbol of "power or omnipotence. . . . A girl wants it for the powers which it symbolizes and the freedom it promises from her previous sense of dependence, and not because it is inherently and obviously better to be masculine" (123). As Lydia gains that knowledge and experience, her dependence on Branson decreases, shifting to an increasingly romantic relationship as Lydia remedies her "lack." It could be said that when she and Branson finally end up in bed in *Sacrilege,* she is seeking a child from the father.

Lydia's own family is mentioned only in passing until *Sacrilege* when there is some consideration of the influence her great-grandmother, Granny Abby, had on the molding of her character and her choice of career. Lydia has chosen defense work partly in defiance of Granny Abby's strong opinions about what should be done with murderers; still Granny Abby approved of her choice, believing that Lydia should make up her own mind and not always follow the advice of her elders (*Sacrilege* 136). Granny Abby is Lydia's only mother figure, illustrating Chodorow's theories about the ambivalent relationship between mothers and adolescent daughters. And so Lydia turns to Branson.

Even her name, Fairchild, not only refers to Lydia's good looks, which are noted by all who often relegate her to the position of ornament to Branson, but also suggests a patriarchal/paternalistic relationship, implying that she needs the care of an "adult." The relationship is typical of the patriarchy: Branson is the authority figure to whom Lydia must refer for guidance. Their first interview in *Impulse* establishes this father-daughter relationship when he concludes, paternalistically, that she is "worth saving" because of her outstanding academic record and promise for a career in law (8-10).

Branson is not the only patriarchal figure in Lydia's life. She has been sent to Canadian, Texas, from Southern Methodist University by the dean of the Law School who is concerned that her extracurricular activities may endanger her law school career. According to Branson, the dean said "that you were a sucker for a worthless man and you were going to ruin your . . . I believe his words were 'Goddamned career if somebody didn't teach her to look for nettles among the roses'" (10-11). Not surprisingly, Lydia is not amused by this criticism.

Branson is the embodiment of Jane Gallop's insistence that the patriarchy is "grounded in the uprightness of the father. If he were devious and unreliable, he could not have the power to legislate. The law is supposed to be just—that is, impartial, indifferent, free from desire" (75). An attorney, Branson is not only an officer of the law, but personally, by his very being, he *is* the law, the perfectly "impartial, indifferent, free from desire" father figure, sometimes devious, but never unreliable, echoing Lacan's Law of the Father.

The aspect of Branson's character which is free from desire does change over the course of the series, as he responds to Lydia. In *Impulse* he informs her that "although you are beautiful, quite desirable in fact, I have no designs on your body. It is your mind I plan to seduce" (11). In Lydia's response Meredith parodies the romance: "You're going to save me from my evil companions and, being above the sins of the flesh, you promise not to seduce me as part of my salvation. In return, I'm to control my romantic tendencies and not fall in love with you" (13). In *Murder by Deception* the matter of romance between them arises relatively briefly: once she cuddles up to him after realizing that they may have indeed been in the presence of the murderer and on another occasion she thinks that there is "something exciting about having a knight in shining armor (or embroidered silk vest) engage in combat on your behalf" (226). In this novel the sexual tension between lawyer and clerk is less important than in *Impulse*. By the third novel, *Murder by Masquerade*, however, she sits in his lap, declaring her intention to kiss him; because she has just discovered another body, her action and his less-than-reluctant response are excused.

Fairchild and Branson are often stereotyped in the series. She reacts emotionally to situations while Branson reacts in the stereotypically logical male fashion. Indeed, their ways of addressing each other convey this dichotomy. She calls him "John Lloyd" but he refers to her as "Miss Fairchild" until in some moment of stress, usually when she is in danger, he shifts to "Lydia." She attempts to break down the intellectual and experiential distance between them, while he strives to maintain it. Her insistence on using his first name may be what Lorraine Cade refers to as a difficulty of knowing the difference between authoritative and authoritarian. Cade notes that women are supposed to have a problem in giving trust because of their beliefs in their "lack of rational capacity"—beliefs which enforce paternalistic control (185-86). Branson frequently appeals to Lydia's rationality and just as frequently acts as if he doubts that she possesses the quality; Meredith often allows Lydia to act as if she does indeed lack "rational capacity."

In the beginning of their relationship in *Impulse*, Lydia appears to have good cause for her difficulty with placing trust when Branson uses her striking resemblance to a supposedly dead woman to shock the woman's family. Lydia's reaction—shock and a decidedly cold shoulder turned toward him—has justification; she and the others have been manipulated. Branson's rejoinder is paternalistically patronizing. He calls her attitude "stereotypically feminine" and when she replies, "How do you expect me to act? Like a man?" he continues that her behavior is "inappropriately juvenile" (72). But his superior attitude is justified in the Freudian scheme because he is not only older and wiser but he also possesses what she lacks, the phallus of knowledge and experience.

Over the course of the first four novels Lydia gains experience, most notably in *Masquerade*, when she openly defies Branson to go undercover as a hooker. Later, when she is undercover officially and attacked by the killer, she is able to defend herself without Branson's help: she has killed the killer by the time he and the police arrive. Although the trauma of the event carries over into the fourth novel, *Murder by Reference,* as Lydia blocks memory of what actually happened, here she is not a victim as she was when shot in *Impulse* and struck on the head in *Deception*. In neither of those attacks does she see or know her attacker. But in *Masquerade* she fights and knows whom she is fighting. She gains a measure of independence through the experience in spite of the physical and mental trauma that she suffers.

In another element of the Freudian scheme, women not only relate to and envy their fathers but, along with possessing "weak superegos and deficient moral sense," women are considered "competitively hostile towards other women and envious of men" (Gardiner, "Mind Mother" 117).[3] While it cannot be said that Lydia's superego and moral sense are problematic, her progress through the series begins at the point of competitive hostility and envy, progressing to a far less Freudian position by the third and fourth novels. In *Murder by Impulse*, Lydia feels inadequate beside Christy Steele, the "pocket size Venus" (44), and genuinely hostile toward Amy Steele whom she resembles so closely. Beside Christy she feels awkward; she simply detests the malicious and manipulative Amy. And although she genuinely sympathizes with the disfigured Cammie, there is still an element of jealousy because Cammie and Branson have a "past." In the second novel she sympathizes with Frances's daughter Rachel. But her competitive hostility is reserved for

Elizabeth Thornton, a strikingly beautiful woman, who also shares a "past" with Branson.

The third novel, *Murder by Masquerade,* brings a change from the jealousy and hostility of the first two. Lydia's sympathies and feminist inclinations are engaged by the prostitutes from Amarillo Boulevard, while her ire is aroused by an "activist" acquaintance who

embraced every cause from A to W, anti-apartheid to whales. . . . Unhampered by logic or consistency, she could argue in favor of two opposing viewpoints, often simultaneously. Theoretically she was a master politician in embryo. Practically her personality would have made St. Francis turn to poisoning pigeons and setting snares. (48-49)

When the activist tries to recruit Lydia for a demonstration against a brewery, Lydia decides she must return to Amarillo to seek the identity of the Butcher. In this, she is not competing with the prostitutes but connecting with them. After all, they do not share a past with Branson.

In *Murder by Reference* female competitiveness surfaces again. Fortunately, the super competent, self-assured museum director, Rachel Applebaum, does have "a narrow run in one leg of her panty hose, which saved Lydia from feeling completely inferior" (*Reference* 105). Inferiority complex aside, Lydia's hostility is directed not toward Rachel Applebaum but Monique Whitney, the complete bitch, who Lydia suspects "last appeared in her natural state at birth" (*Reference* 18). In *Sacrilege* the actual murderer, Mildred Fisher, demonstrates definite jealousy of Lydia, calling her a "harlot" although Lydia does not return the feeling (*Sacrilege* 142).

In all of her relationships with women, however casual, Lydia is "mentored" by John Lloyd Branson's words of wisdom. Nowhere is this mentoring by the wise father more evident than in *Masquerade*. When Lydia angrily confronts Branson for what she perceives as his lack of concern for a murdered prostitute, he tells her:

Your very physical appearance, your hopes and aspirations, the fact you have a future while they have none, is a reproach to them. . . . They will not respond to your goodness. They will perceive you as an interloper, a troublemaker, and they already have enough troubles for a lifetime. (45)

Branson's words demonstrate Cade's assertion that "perfect, objective knowledge of other people is not possible" (39). Lydia, he tells her, does not know the prostitutes and cannot understand them, no matter how much she sympathizes with their plight. The memory of his assessment, along with her confrontation with the activist acquaintance, sends Lydia to the Boulevard to show the true "feminine solidarity" to which she had paid lip service earlier (*Masquerade* 26).

This action seems to represent a turning point in Lydia's development. She demonstrates Gardiner's observation that women define themselves "through social relationships; issues of fusion and merger of the self with others are significant" ("On Female Identity" 182). She feels compelled to take action on behalf of the Amarillo Boulevard prostitutes both because she is a feminist and because she must defy Branson. As she begins to define herself she begins to separate from Branson, to develop other relationships. Up to this point she has made many attempts to strike out on her own, but none have been totally successful. In fact, these attempts have been more expressions of immature rebellion than serious forays into independent action. The actions that she takes and the resultant knocks that she receives in *Masquerade* give her a new perspective on independence. After being "evicted from the foulest bar on Amarillo Boulevard" for punching out one of the bar's customers who is taking her up on her disguise as a Boulevard hooker, she muses:

the old Lydia would have marched back into the Bimbo Bar and flattened the bartender, or at least attempted to flatten him.

The Old Lydia was an immature, impulsive fool.

The new Lydia was cautious.

The old Lydia would have had to be tossed out of the Bimbo in pieces, screaming defiance as each part of her landed in the dirt.

The new Lydia sat very quietly on the step. . . .

. . .

Lydia decided becoming a mature, responsible adult was a demoralizing process. (*Masquerade* 106)

This reaction seems like just another lesson learned the hard way. But it differs from lessons in the previous novels because it is Lydia on her own who realizes what has happened. She has not had Branson to tell her.

However, it would appear that Meredith is not certain about allowing the father-daughter relationship between Lydia and Branson to be resolved just yet, for later in the novel when Lydia is arrested and charged with murder, Branson comes riding to her rescue. Lydia admits to him that "maybe wisdom isn't part of my basic personality profile" (*Masquerade* 151). She reacts like a frustrated romance heroine or a child: "When I say you . . . looking like some some kind of avenging angel, I thought, like the fool I am, that you came because it was me, Lydia Fairchild, a particular fool, in trouble, and not because you'd come to the rescue of any child or fool in general" (153). Here Lydia shows herself to be the stereotypical Freudian or romance-novel female, needing to be rescued by the wise father. Meredith clearly accepts Cade's assertion that subjectivity is a female trait and objectivity male (35).

Immediately after Lydia's outburst Branson reveals that, believing her to be in danger, he has tracked her from Dallas to the Boulevard. He has lost his objectivity, a disconcerting experience: "I am as distressed over my own behavior on this occasion as I am by yours," he tells her. "Your irresponsible impulsiveness must be contagious" (154-55). In typical male fashion he has constructed her as "man's contradiction, and at the same time often construct[ed] her *as* a contradiction—incoherent, mercurial, nonsensical," as Langbauer says in her study of gender in the English novel, *Women and Romance*. "The other [the woman] is what allows the subject to construct a self at all, to seem to resolve its own incoherence and contradictions" (4). Lydia's subjectivity, which Branson wishes to turn into lawyerly objectivity, has replaced his objectivity, at least momentarily, as he demonstrates a whole range of "incoherence and contradictions" that he has assigned to Lydia; and he works very hard at returning to his former properly male behavior. Nonetheless, later in the novel, his concern for her safety reveals that these subjective qualities are not merely a momentary aberration.

During the crucial scene between Lydia and *Masquerade*'s killer, Louis Bryant, a newspaper reporter who believes himself the reincarnation of Jack the Ripper, she does appear to retreat from her totally independent mode. She cries out once for John Lloyd to help her; it is understandable that she would call out for a specific person who has in the past rescued her. But more important than what could be considered a retreat from her position of growing independence from Branson is what she tells Bryant about his game with Branson. When Bryant calls her "the thing he [Branson] values most" she replies: "I'm not a thing, I'm a person" and "Your controlling me has nothing to do with John Lloyd. Because I'm human too, not an object. I'm playing in this game, and I think it's boring" (*Masquerade* 230). As Lydia attempts to shock her attacker to his senses, she is also asserting her own selfhood, defining her own identity. This moment of crisis is not, however, typically female as Gardiner views it, noting that the "female counterpart of male identity crisis may occur more diffusely, at a different stage or not at all" ("On Female Identity" 184). Being trapped in a room with a killer intent on making her his next victim is hardly "diffuse." Lydia's subsequent repression of the experience, trying to deny the fear that she cannot escape even though the Butcher is dead, does serve as a diffusing factor. The crisis is not actually over until she faces her fears.

In the following novel, *Murder by Reference,* Meredith shows a Lydia who has not yet recovered from her experiences with Bryant. Branson tries to play both therapist and father; he tries to force her to remember what happened. He insists, "Your account [of the killing] at the time we found you with the body was curiously incomplete" (74). In a scene whose style echoes the romance novel, she rejects his offer of help when he says:

"You must [remember]. Your fear of remembering is like a cancer; it is consuming your strength, impoverishing your spirit. It is killing you! Feel my strength, Lydia," he said, pulling her closer. "I will not let you walk that dark passage of memory alone. Lean on me! Trust me! Tell me! Remember!"

. . .

[She] knew that whatever else they might be to each other, they would never be equals. Not as long as she depended on him for her strength instead of finding it within herself. Dark passages were meant to be walked alone. He could wait at the other end. (75)

During *Reference* Lydia takes every opportunity to walk alone. When she finally faces her problem she is alone in a locked room with the ghost of the Butcher.

As she confronts her ghost, reliving the horror of the night she killed him, he reminds her of what she has to lose: "Only John Lloyd," the Butcher says, ". . . you can't have us both, and you need me. As long as you have me, you'll never have to face the truth, but John Lloyd won't let you hide, will he?" Facing the ghost, she sees herself in the Butcher's eyes and "remembered what she'd fought so hard to forget. With a ragged sigh she accepted the truth about her own nature: given sufficient provocation, she could kill without regret, but worse than that, be glad she did it" (155). After conquering the ghost she realizes that she is now Branson's equal: "she'd walked down her dark passage and conquered fear" (175). She reveals her new knowledge to Branson: "I discovered that the memory I feared wasn't of killing the Butcher; it was of remembering that I was glad I killed him. I was afraid of facing that fact about myself" (176). Branson, of course, reassures her that she has simply conquered the guilt a good person should feel about killing: "You killed your ghost when he became the symbol of evil instead of a symbol of your guilty conscience. . . . it demonstrates that you are a sensible young woman who does not intend to allow herself to be a victim, even metaphorically" (177).

Lydia has not simply conquered her guilt. She has killed the father. The Butcher has become the embodiment of that which has controlled her, and by killing his ghost she has freed herself. This also frees her from the father-daughter relationship with Branson, making her his equal. The ghost was right; she could not have both him and John Lloyd, John Lloyd as equal. She could have John Lloyd as father, but their relationship has progressed beyond the paternalistic to the romantic, something both of them recognize. For the romance to develop, however, Lydia must be equal to him, not dependent upon him.

With this knowledge, Lydia is now free to solve the mystery. When Bill Whitney confesses not only to the current murder but to one committed twenty years ago, Branson accepts his old friend's confession. Lydia, no longer part of Branson, can see that "the references are all wrong" (*Reference* 244-45). She recognizes that Whitney's killing of the witness to the old murder was accidental and that he has been protecting an innocent person whom he thought was guilty for twenty years. Branson is too close to the entire sequence of events to realize that "the references are all wrong," but Lydia now can as she could not before killing her ghost.

Lydia's independence from Branson is not as fully realized as it would seem at the end of *Reference*. In *Sacrilege* she seems to be taking at least one step backward for every two she has taken forward. Once again she is denied the solution to the mystery, although she believes she knows and declares so publicly, only to be proven wrong by Branson. Even more problematic for Lydia's development is the fact that Branson chooses not to confide in her regarding his method of defense.

Branson accepts the job of defending the minister accused of murdering his new wife and committing sacrilege by placing her body in the church nativity scene without considering Lydia's opinion. To her this is a sign that he still does not accept her as his equal, a point of real importance to her. When she confronts him, he asks if he has disillusioned her or "merely" hurt her pride. Her answer sums up the often thorny relationship between them:

You hurt me—period. I thought I had won my spurs, so to speak, when I helped you solve the murder at the Panhandle Plains Museum [*Reference*]. I thought I'd made it. I thought I'd earned my place beside you, but now you're acting like you expect me to walk two paces to the rear again. I may be a little flawed in some respects, but I don't deserve that kind of treatment. (28)

When Lydia says that she "helped" him solve the murder in the museum, she is backing away from asserting herself, from declaring her equality and independence. As the scene continues Lydia's subordinate position is again emphasized through her response to a simple command: "John Lloyd Branson had a way of commanding obedience that required more strength of character to resist than Lydia possessed. . . . It was another inequity in their relationship" (*Sacrilege* 29).

Branson continues to exclude Lydia from his deliberations. He attempts to justify his actions in the courtroom to her by explaining that he has "never shared confidences with a woman before" although he has had relationships whose "limits were clearly defined." He admits that "I have always weighed my legal strategies in solitude and must learn to do otherwise. It is an unsettling experience for me" (159-60). Nevertheless, he continues to act without confiding in or explaining to her, leading to further heated discussions of trust. She accuses him of "stealing" her trust, her belief in him, which leads to her resigning from his employ (196).

Later, when they literally kiss and make up, one of her demands is that he treat her as an equal. She reminds him that "you used my own principles, my own belief in justice, against me. You turned me into a performing monkey" and when he cites necessity she replies "I *am* a bad liar and not a very good actress, and you did ask me to trust you, but that doesn't excuse you. Not once—*not once*—did you say you were sorry" (*Sacrilege* 217). Branson reminds her that he had warned her and, in romance novel language, continues: "You expect me to take you to my bosom, never knowing when you're going to sink your viperous fangs in my heart?" To which she replies: "Yes. And I expect one more thing. I expect you to never use me again as a *thing* like David Hailey did to his wife in the name of some undefined, unexplained higher purpose" (*Sacrilege* 218). Branson has indeed used her, as he has in previous novels, and she has objected before. In this situation, however, his deviousness is more problematic because Lydia has changed after solving the mystery in *Reference*. When she finally believes that she can stand on equal footing with him, when she believes she has gained the phallus of knowledge and experience, he withdraws his approval and his recognition of her abilities in the name of necessity. She has invested her trust in him, believing that it is a rational choice, while it is actually mostly emotional, but he does not reciprocate.

In the epilogue to *Sacrilege*, Lydia presents her idea of the criminal's identity with confidence born of her success in *Reference* and is proven wrong. Again she expresses her shaken confidence: "Is that always the way it's going to be? I talk and you listen. Then I make a fool of myself, which you knew all along I would do, and you leap in with the right answer and look wise." He attempts to reassure her that he had not been sure of his own identification of the murderer and didn't want to "cast doubt" on her because her deductions were "more reasonable, more rational, more scientific, and more consistent with the evidence." He assures her that he would not embarrass her in public (274-45). His assurances sound hollow and even patronizing. In spite of their now obviously romantic relationship, the father-daughter relationship is still paramount: she is still not equal.

The formulaic paternalism of the romance subverts the developing equality of a more contemporary model of male-female relationship. Even before Branson's attempt to placate her in the epilogue, his lavish Christmas gifts of jewelry and clothes indicate a paternal rather than a professional and equal relationship: even the lingerie fits perfectly and the suit he gives her is turquoise blue rather than a more "lawyerly" navy or gray.

Lydia Fairchild is both an appealing and appalling character to a feminist reader. In the first two books of the series her rash feminism can be annoying, but as she begins to assert her independence in a real fashion with more than lip service to feminist ideals in *Masquerade,* she becomes a more appealing character. As she continues to grow in *Reference* the feminist reader has hope that Lydia will come into her own, will gain equity with Branson. Since the first four novels of the series, *Murder*[s] *by Impulse, Deception, Masquerade,* and *Reference,* lead in this direction, the reader assumes that she will succeed. With a return to the father-daughter relationship in spite of the consummated romance in *Sacrilege,* one wonders what the sixth novel of the series will bring or even if there will be one.

Notes

1. Meredith mentioned in particular a beauty queen with her own tool belt who fixed things around the bookstore as a model for Lydia (Personal Interview).

2. Interestingly, *The Sheriff and the Pheasant Hunt Murders*, part of another series, is dedicated to "the 7,999 gentlemen and one male chauvinist pig whom I accompanied on the 1984 pheasant hunt in Moore County, Texas" (n.p.).

3. Chodorow disagrees on this point, saying "there is little to suggest either that penis envy completely permeates women's lives, or that the envy, jealousy, vanity, and pettiness that supposedly result from penis envy are characteristic of women" (165).

Works Cited

Cade, Lorraine. *What Can She Know? Feminist Theory and the Construction of Knowledge.* Ithaca: Cornell UP. 1991.

Chodorow, Nancy. *The Reproduction of Mothering: Psychoanalysis and the Sociology of Gender.* Berkeley: California UP, 1978.

Gallop, Jane. *The Daughter's Seduction: Feminism and Psychoanalysis.* Ithaca: Cornell UP, 1982.

Gardiner, Judith Kegan, "Mind Mother: Psychoanalysis and Feminism." *Making a Difference: Feminist Literary Criticism.* Ed. Gayle Greene and Coppelia Kahn. London: Methuen, 1985. 113-45.

——. "On Female Identity and Writing by Women." *Writing and Sexual Difference.* Ed. Elizabeth Abel. Chicago: Chicago UP, 1982. 177-92.

Langbauer, Laurie. *Women and Romance: The Consolations of Gender in the English Novel.* Ithaca: Cornell UP, 1990.

Meredith, D.R. *Murder by Deception.* New York: Ballantine, 1989.

——. *Murder by Impulse.* New York: Ballantine, 1987.

——. *Murder by Masquerade.* New York: Ballantine, 1990.

——. *Murder by Reference.* New York: Ballantine, 1991.

——. *Murder by Sacrilege.* New York: Ballantine, 1993.

——. *The Sheriff and the Pheasant Hunt Murders.* New York: Ballantine, 1993.

——. *Personal interview* (at book signing). 21 Jan. 1993.

The Decline of Hilda Adams

Mary P. Freier

Mary Roberts Rinehart's Hilda Adams stories and novels indicate a great deal of tension in Rinehart's own view of her profession. Although she always espoused a traditional role for women, she herself had, more or less by accident, taken on a most untraditional role as breadwinner of the family, despite the fact that her husband was a doctor. Much of Rinehart's public persona was based on her being a working mother, as Robert H. Davis's "sketch" shows. However, much as Rinehart enjoyed both her work and her family, she was aware that she had chosen an untraditional path. This tension is shown throughout the series, as Hilda Adams becomes more discontented with her own work, and therefore less powerful in dealing with the problems that confront her.

Rinehart herself trained as a nurse, but never worked as one, since, as Jan Cohn's biography explains, she met her husband during her training and became engaged before she finished nursing college. But even this bare biographical fact seems to be a source of tension for Rinehart; Dr. Stanley Rinehart had to challenge the regulations that forbade doctors to fraternize with probationary nurses by demanding permission to take Mary out. They were married two years later, and the whole hospital celebrated with them (*My Story* 68). However, there was now no question of Mary ever practicing nursing.

Rinehart's nursing training taught her a great deal about the less pleasant aspects of life, not only from her work in the hospital, but because probationers were sent out to the poorer neighborhoods of Pittsburgh to take care of sick people who could not afford private nursing (*My Story* 74). Despite these experiences, Rinehart deliberately avoided realism. She wrote of her early work,

I knew better than the average the weaknesses of mankind, the errors; I had seen human relations at their most naked, human emotions when the bars were down and the soul peered out, heroic, cowardly or defiant. Yet I could not write of these things. I did not want to recall them. . . . But in writing I was seeking escape, as other women had sought it in other ways. I wanted escape from remembering, for remembering frightened me. I turned to romance, to crime, to farce, to adventure; anything but reality." (*My Story* 89-90)

129

In a way, by writing about a nurse-detective, Rinehart confronts the realism that she had sought to avoid. However, Hilda Adams is also looking for an escape; she turns to detecting as a release from "institutional work, with its daily round of small worries, its monotonous years, with my soul gradually shrinking and shaping itself to fit a set of rules" ("Buckled Bag" 10).

One of Rinehart's major premises for using a nurse as a detective was the fact that nurses learn a great deal from their patients, often about things that they never really wanted to know. Rinehart wrote in her biography of serving on a women's ward, and said that, as her patients got well,

They would hold me, or the other nurses, by the arm and pour out their life stories. Sometimes they told things they had never told before. We nurses were like nuns to them, sometimes like priests. They wanted to confess, to open their tired hearts. It gave them relief. . . . Things were brought out into the open of which I had never dreamed. (*My Story* 54-55)

One gets the feeling that Rinehart might also have preferred never to have known of these things, for Hilda Adams says of these stories,

One way and another [the doctor and clergyman] get the story. . . . They get it, but they do not want it. They cannot use it. . . . She [the trained nurse] does not want it [the story] either . . . but unless she's a fool she ends by holding the family secret in the hollow of her hand. It worries her. She needs her hands. She gets rid of it as soon as she can and forgets about it. ("Buckled Bag" 7)

What makes Hilda Adams and Mary Roberts Rinehart different is the methods that they choose to rid themselves of these stories: Hilda Adams chooses to use her information to help catch criminals; Rinehart tried to avoid hers by writing crime and romance novels.

The Hilda Adams stories and novels are particularly interesting in a study of Rinehart, since they were published over a span of nearly thirty years, and Hilda Adams was Rinehart's only series detective. "The Buckled Bag" and "Locked Doors" were serialized in 1914, and reprinted in an omnibus volume in 1933. *Miss Pinkerton* was serialized and published in 1932, eighteen years later. *Haunted Lady* was serialized and published in 1942, ten years after *Miss Pinkerton*. Rinehart herself went through many changes in this period, and it is not surprising that Hilda Adams changes in this period, too. Indeed, Hilda reflects Rinehart's disillusionment brought about by two world wars and her own widowhood. The Hilda of *Haunted Lady* contrasts sharply with the Hilda of "The Buckled Bag"; she has lost her self-confidence and her ability to trust her own judgment.

In the beginning of the series, Hilda is not only single, she is competent and happy. In the early stories, many of her patients comment on her competence and strength, and her independence prevents her being dominated, either professionally or romantically, by her police supervisor, Inspector Patton. However, in the three-decade span of the series, Hilda ages nine years. By the final novel, *Haunted Lady,* there is a strong sense of Hilda's having lived thirty years in nine; she is tired and seems to want to relinquish her independence. Hilda even seems to be in danger of losing her identity as a trained nurse in *Haunted Lady*; she succumbs to Patton's romantic advances, and the strong and confident protagonist of the early stories is left confused and flustered.

Throughout the series, Hilda must deal with her own ethical concerns about using her nursing profession as an opportunity to gather information for the police. In "The Buckled Bag," she admits that "I hated it in the beginning" (8). She realizes that she is taking advantage of her position as a nurse: "A nurse gets under the very skin of the soul. She finds a mind surrendered" (8). Later, in "Locked Doors," she uses the same terminology: "a trained nurse gets under the very skin of the soul" (56). She also claims to have settled her own ethical questions: "if the criminal uses every means against society, why not society against the criminal?" She admits, however, "At first I had used this as a flag of truce to my nurse's ethical training; now I flaunted it, a mental and moral banner. The criminal against society, and I against the criminal!" But her justification is strangely contradictory; she claims to "[heal] pain by augmenting it sometimes, but working like a surgeon, for good" (56). She assists this rationalization with a reminder that she has never allowed her nursing to suffer from her detection, that her patients' needs as patients have always come first (56).

However, as time passes, Hilda begins to doubt her logic. Although she continues her defense of her combination of professions in *Miss Pinkerton,* she has begun to have serious questions about it: "To tell the truth, I was wondering why I continued my work for the police. One way and another I had run a good many risks for them and lost a lot of sleep." Although she does not think that she has broken faith with her patients, she has literally been doing double duty: "I had used hours when I needed rest to help solve some piece of wickedness or other" (94). The case in *Miss Pinkerton* especially frustrates Hilda, because she must alter her views of nursing (and probably of detection) as being God-like ("since it is His peace which we try to bring"). Her inability to help in this case is due to her patient's refusal to tell her story, and her frustration is focused on her detecting: "I began to resent my place in that house, with its spying and watching" (*Miss Pinkerton* 116). Later, her frustration is compounded, when she has earned her patient's gratitude, although her confidence is not: "And once again I detested my job, sneaking into that house under false pretenses and fooling the poor old creature into being even mildly grateful to me. I had to harden myself deliberately . . . before I felt equal to going on with the work" (*Miss Pinkerton* 124). By *Haunted Lady,* she tells Patton, "I hate this job. . . . I hate prying and spying. I'm through. I can't go on" (378).

It seems clear that Hilda's original motivation for taking on the double role was a sense of control over her own life and thrill-seeking (she admits to finding "the criminal . . . absorbing" ["Buckled Bag" 8]). But by taking on an ethically questionable role, she creates a great deal of tension for herself.

Rinehart's writing also caused her to take on two careers: the career of author and the career of housewife and mother. In the first third of the twentieth century there was no discussion of men helping their wives with housework and child care, and, even when Stanley Rinehart gave up his medical practice, he did so only to become Mary's business manager. While her writing offered her the escape that she desired and probably needed, it also gave her very little time to rest and put her in conflict with social norms, not a comfortable position for Mary Roberts Rinehart, who was no radical.

In 1914, Rinehart seems to have dispelled any discomfort in her dual role by presenting her working woman as unmarried. Hilda's sense of professionalism and her identification of herself with her profession give her great confidence in herself and inspired confidence in others. In her first nursing-detective case, Mrs. March, her nervous patient, remarks, "How big and strong and competent you look!" ("Buckled Bag" 16), despite the fact that Hilda is consistently described as small. In her second case, Mrs. Reed tells her "How fresh you always look! . . . And so self-reliant. I wish I had your courage" ("Locked Doors" 73). A great deal of Hilda's strength comes from her identity as a nurse. She is very proud of her profession, and often remarks on the reactions of others to her profession. She comments on the fact that old servants resent the presence of a "trained" nurse in the house (*Miss Pinkerton* 101). It is as if one of Rinehart's purposes in writing these stories and novels was to make people aware that nurses are professionals. Hilda's initial reaction to the case in "Locked Doors," where the Reeds want a nurse for their children in a house with no servants is one of resentment: "No servants! A good many people think a trained nurse is a sort of upper servant. I've been in houses where they were amazed to discover that I was a college woman and, finding the two things irreconcilable, have openly accused me of having been driven to such a desperate course as hospital training by an unfortunate love affair" (58). The thought that a woman could choose a profession might have rankled slightly with Rinehart, who had originally hoped to become a doctor, a career goal that she had to modify because of family finances (*My Story* 38).

However, Hilda's pride in her work seems to diminish in *Miss Pinkerton*; she is unable to deal with a case of carbon-monoxide poisoning, in part because of her lack of experience, and in part because she has just been attacked and is too weak. By *Haunted Lady,* her sense of identity as a nurse has been shattered. At one point another character accuses her of being a policewoman, and she is described as feeling "inadequate and useless" (296). Her sense of failure is also mentioned. Hilda has lost control of the situation—when she goes out, a photographer snaps her picture, and is even insolent to her.

The relationship between Hilda and Inspector Patton similarly alters throughout the series. At the beginning of the series, Hilda is very much in control; by the end she has lost control, both personally and professionally. Hilda and Patton's relationship is ostensibly a professional one, although Patton often flirts with Hilda and indicates that he finds her attractive. She, however, does not respond to his advances until the end of *Haunted Lady,* thus relinquishing any control that she may have had in the relationship.

Patton controls the relationship professionally, primarily because it is he who assigns Hilda's cases. However, early in the series he is also a mentor of sorts for Hilda, who, in many ways, has no idea of what she is getting into. Before she begins her work for Patton, Hilda's notions of the crimes that she will be dealing with are wild and romantic, so much so that she realizes a "disappointment" when Patton tells her about her first case: "nothing but the bloodiest sort of crime would have come up to my expectation. Certainly nothing less than a murder had been in my thoughts." Hilda is also puzzled about her function as a nurse-detective: "if you are going to ask me to put myself in her place, and try to imagine what could have happened, and to follow her mental processes, I can't do it." Patton explains that he only wants "a little inside help." He wants her to gain the trust of the family, who will not talk to the police because of "family pride" ("Buckled Bag" 14). Patton eventually makes her buy a revolver and warns her about potentially dangerous behavior.

Hilda's performance alters with her experience; at first her value to Patton is due to her professional role, but by *Haunted Lady,* her personal qualities have taken over, as Patton explains to the new commissioner: "She looks as though she still thought the stork brought babies. . . . But she can see more with those blue eyes of hers than most of us could with a microscope. What's more, people confide in her. She's not the talking sort, so they think she's safe" (237). Hilda, however, often wonders what she is supposed to do, and what her real value is: "I often think . . . my only real value to him . . . [is] to use me as an opportunity to think out loud" (*Miss Pinkerton* 108).

Although Patton is said to "respect" her (*Haunted Lady* 261), he gets very angry when she does not agree with him about a case or does not reveal information to him. He even goes so far on these occasions as to make sexist remarks, like those in *Miss Pinkerton*: "Well, that comes of letting a woman in on a thing like this. She gets carried away by her emotions" (169). In *Haunted Lady,* he complains, "Everybody around here knows something—except me. Even you, probably. . . . I wouldn't put it past you, you know. You've held out on me before." When Hilda suggests that it might be "necessary" for her to withhold information, he reacts angrily: "'God damn it, Hilda,' he roared, 'if I thought you had any pets around here and were protecting them, I'd—I'd turn you over my knee'" (313). He often refers to her as "little," and sees her appearance as childlike (*Haunted Lady* 237), so this threat fits his view of her. It does not, however, fit Hilda's early self-image, for when she does not behave in a calm and collected manner she is ashamed of herself as a "shivering girl" ("Locked Doors" 76).

Part of Patton's anger is due to the fact that he perceives Hilda as a threat to his own ability to control situations: "See here. I'll be damned if I'll have you running this case" (*Haunted Lady* 344). This battle for control is very much apparent in Patton's personal relationship with Hilda.

A good deal of Patton's behavior to Hilda might be construed today as sexual harassment. However, Hilda does not seem to be threatened by it, perhaps because she first met Patton when he was a patient of hers, and she was in control of him. Her comment on his behavior at this time is that he "had never attempted any sentimentalities with me, which is more than can be said for the usual convalescent male over forty" ("Buckled Bag" 9). Obviously, Hilda has encountered flirtatious patients before, and knows very well how to deal with them, a characterization that seems to come from Rinehart's own nursing experience. In her autobiography, Rinehart explains, "Now and then a man in a private room wanted to hold my hand, but I was extremely firm about this unless he was very ill" (*My Story* 69). So Patton is not considered a sexual or romantic threat at the beginning of the series.

However, in the second story, "Locked Doors," Patton, no longer bedridden, begins to assert himself more. The case requires Hilda to masquerade as a nurse from a particular hospital, where a different uniform is worn, one that includes a bonnet with lawn ties. Patton remarks that, although he is usually "afraid of your chin . . . the white lawn ties have a softening effect." He implies that he might have the courage to kiss her, but decides that "the chin is there, ties or no ties" (73). He also tries, not very subtly, to discover Hilda's romantic status: "There's probably a young man somewhere who will come gunning for me if anything happens to you." Hilda's response is hardly encouraging: "'There is no young man,' I said shortly" (84).

Hilda actually solves this mystery because of her nursing expertise, and Patton does acknowledge her contribution. However, he must try to regain control soon after. In order to find out if Hilda has any affection for him, he suggests that he has been bitten by a plague-ridden ferret. Hilda responds with shock, and Patton comments, "The chin . . . is not so firm as I had thought. The outlines are savage, but the dimple . . . You poor little thing; are you really frightened?" Hilda, quite naturally, responds angrily to this cheap trick, and the story concludes: "He stood for a time looking down at me; then, unexpectedly, he bent over and touched his lips to my bandaged arm. . . . Then he tiptoed out of the room. His back was very sheepish" (92). Hilda has clearly won this particular battle for control, although she has revealed that she would care if Patton were to die of plague.

The ending of "Locked Doors" is typical of the series, where the stories and novels end with similar romantic sparring. At the end of *Miss Pinkerton,* Patton virtually proposes marriage: "I suppose she knows that there is one case she can have for life. . . . A very long and hard case, involving a life sentence, chains and what have you" (234-35). Hilda does not respond, and again we are left with the sense that she still controls her own life and choices.

However, by *Haunted Lady,* Hilda and Patton's relationship has changed. Hilda seems to be lacking in self-confidence in general, and Patton is much more free in his flirtatious references. He emphasizes her marital status when talking to the commissioner about her, and he constantly notes her appearance. He expresses concern about the possibility of Hilda falling in love: "I—we can't afford to lose you, you know" (282). After a discussion of the case, he once again offers to kiss her, but she deflects him (346). He even comments at one point that Hilda is essentially a "domestic creature" (381).

By the end of the novel, Hilda has capitulated to him, although her discouragement with her profession and self-image have more to do with it than her affection for Patton. When Patton suggests marriage and the possibility of his calling on her, her response is, "I'd prefer even that to being left alone." Her attitude after he leaves shows less of the happy and excited lover than the defeated woman. When she hears the phone ring and knows that the call is from Patton, "She looked desperately about her, at the books she wanted to read, at her soft bed, and through the door to her small cheerful sitting room with the bird sleeping in its cage. Then she picked up the receiver." When her fears are confirmed at the sound of Patton's voice, she is "instantly covered with confusion" (382).

Part of the reason for this acquiescence on Hilda's part seems to be based on her need for sentiment. Sentiment is important to Hilda, but by the end of the series she is no longer able to settle for it "vicariously." In "The Buckled Bag," Hilda refuses payment for her work because the sight of the young lovers restored to one another is satisfaction enough. Patton finds this odd, and Hilda responds, "I've taken most of my pleasures and all of my sentiment vicariously for a number of years. . . . And, even if it's the other person's, sentiment one has to have!" (54). But Hilda is not always happy with vicarious sentiment. When she takes the case at the Reeds' in "Locked Doors," she looks at their happy marriage with longing: "It made me feel homesick for the home I didn't have. I've had the same feeling before, of being a rank outsider—a sort of defrauded feeling. I've had it when I've seen the look in a man's eyes when his wife comes to after an operation. And I've had it, for that matter, when I've put a new baby in its mother's arms for the first time. I had it for sure that morning, while she slept there and he stroked her pretty hair" (69). Her sentimental attitude is also shown when she takes the case for the Fairbanks family in *Haunted Lady*. This family was one of the most important society families when Hilda was a child, and she remembers the wedding of Marian Fairbanks and Frank Garrison very vividly, as she had stood on the street and watched the wedding party when she was a probationer: "To the little probationer outside on the pavement it had been pure romance: Marian and Frank Garrison, clad in youth and beauty that day" (241). The young Hilda takes pleasure in the romantic happiness of others.

Taking vicarious pleasure in bringing lovers together is sentimental, but it is also an assertion of power and a taking control of the "story" that the nurse is told. It should be noted that in a detective novel or story, knowledge of the "story" is absolute power, which in part explains Hilda's and Patton's desire to gather information and occasionally withhold it. Hilda refers to the "story" more than once; it is the thing that fills the nurse's hands so that she cannot do her work, and it is the source of conflict in her professional relationship with Patton: "He wanted no excuses. He wanted the story" (*Haunted Lady* 302). In "Locked Doors,"

Patton refuses to tell Hilda the story, ostensibly because he wants her "to go in with a fresh mind" (55). In *Haunted Lady,* Hilda has literally lost control of the story; her story is being told by a third-person narrator, and not always from her point of view.

"The Buckled Bag" is a story about the addiction to creating stories, which could well refer to Rinehart's own pleasure in creating her fictions, even though she was supposedly writing only to supplement the family income. The story that the nurse is supposed to be told is where Clare March may have gone. While Clare is literally addicted to cocaine, Hilda is addicted to finding out the story. Clare overcomes her addiction for the sake of her lover; Hilda ignores a possible lover for the sake of her addiction.

Hilda begins the story by saying that her health has been poor, because she has been under extra strain for the five years since she has begun working for the police department. She has taken on the extra work for excitement. The desire to know the story is the beginning of Hilda's addiction to detecting; at the beginning of "The Buckled Bag," she describes her second career as "having her by the throat now" (8). Hilda is enthusiastic about her new work at first, so much so that she begins to create the story before Patton gives her any details about her case, and almost rejects the job before she knows what it is. When she finds out about the case, she is disappointed, but as she gets involved in it, she becomes driven to find out the story behind Clare's disappearance. By the end of the story, Hilda is determined to go on with detection, a second career that she has described as being a compulsion and a strain on her health.

Ironically, as Hilda begins her addiction, Clare March overcomes hers. The mystery of the story is Clare's disappearance, and she has disappeared to be cured of her addiction to cocaine. Hilda does not solve this mystery through her nursing knowledge or ratiocination; she is actually told the story by Clare, who, as she has overcome her addiction, can now give up the story, a story that she did not want her parents to know. Clare takes the power of telling the story when Hilda faints and Clare, the patient, then takes care of Hilda, the professional nurse. Hilda comments, "It was curious to see how our positions had been reversed" (50).

Clare explains to Hilda that she was originally given cocaine as a painkiller, but then developed an addiction. She knew that she had to overcome the addiction if she was ever to marry or have children. Hilda, on the other hand, chooses to indulge her addiction, even though she seems to realize that her second career will prevent her having a marriage and children and will require her to have sentiment in her life vicariously.

In "Locked Doors," the story that Hilda is looking for is essentially a Gothic tale. She has been called in to replace a nurse who has "gone to pieces," and the original nurse even says that she thinks murder has been done (55). When Hilda arrives at the Reed home, she learns by her own explorations that there is someone being held in the attic, and, in an interesting twist on *Jane Eyre,* this person turns out to be the French governess. There are suggestions that the problem in the house is ghosts, and, when Hilda goes exploring at night, she encounters what seems to be a disembodied head in a "pointed hood like a monk's cowl" (77). However, the actual mystery is almost purely medical: Mr. Reed is trying to develop a plague serum, and the plague-infected rats that he has been working with have escaped. He has tried to protect his family and neighbors by destroying the middle of a staircase (Hilda's cowled figure is Reed standing up in the wreckage of the staircase in his search of the rats) and searching for the rats at night (hence the rumors of ghosts). The explanation of the governess's presence in the attic is similarly un-Gothic: convinced that she had caught the plague, she would not go to a hospital for fear of getting Reed in trouble and insisted on locking herself away in the attic.

Gothic elements are certainly not foreign to Rinehart's fiction, but Hilda Adams, the practical nurse-detective, seems to have encountered more than her share of them in her four cases. In all of Hilda's cases, she is severely frightened or physically attacked in the course of her investigations. In "The Buckled Bag," she goes to a deserted house to investigate Clare March's story, and is frightened there by Clare herself. This fear is so intense that she continues to have nightmares from it: "I am standing in a dark room and there are stealthy steps drawing nearer and nearer. At last the thing comes toward me; I can hear it; but there is nothing to see. And then it touches me with ice-cold hands—and I waken with a scream" (49). In this encounter, Hilda only faints. However, when she goes down Mr. Reed's gutted staircase, she is not only terrified by Mr. Reed himself, she falls and breaks her arm.

Although Hilda is injured at the Reeds', no one has really meant her any ill will, and her injury is essentially an accident. In *Miss Pinkerton,* however, there are even more frightening incidents and someone actually tries to strangle Hilda. In some ways, this is reminiscent of what Hilda says in "The Buckled Bag" about her addiction to detecting having her by the throat: "just as I opened my mouth to scream, I felt hands close on my throat. I was being slowly strangled from behind. . . . Whoever it was, those hands were prodigiously strong. I was utterly helpless" (221). Hilda does not seem as willing to give herself to her addiction as she was in "The Buckled Bag." In fact, at the beginning of the story she admits that at the time of being strangled, "All I could think of was . . . to get air, to breathe again" (94). There are also more references to possible ghosts in *Miss Pinkerton* than in the first two stories, although ghosts are not the solution to the crime. Hilda seems to be haunted in this novel, possibly by the sacrifices that she has been making for her addiction.

Hilda certainly begins to think about her age in a more negative sense in *Miss Pinkerton* than she has before. In "The Buckled Bag," she tells us that she is twenty-nine, and in "Locked Doors," she announces that it is her thirtieth birthday, and that she is "feeling all of my years" (90). However, in *Miss Pinkerton,* she says "I could see myself in the mirror, and I realized that I looked tired, and older than my age." But she rejects the idea that this work might not be the best thing for her, with its dangers, its nightmares, its aging effects. Instead of quitting, she gets her things together to get back to work on the case: "The game was in my blood, after all" (120).

By *Haunted Lady,* Hilda seems to have given up the romanticism of the Gothic and seems to revert often to her probationer days. When she thinks of taking the job at the Fairbanks house, she remembers watching the Frank Garrison and Marian Fairbanks wedding party as a probationer. The young doctor, Courtney Brooke, "reminded her of [an intern] in the hospital where she had been a probationer. He had found her once in a linen closet and kissed her. It hadn't meant anything, of course. It had been spring, and the windows had been open. She had slapped him" (289). This instance of Hilda's being grabbed from behind is very different from that of *Miss Pinkerton,* and there is a strong sense of nostalgia in this novel. In many ways, Hilda is the haunted lady of the title, haunted by the ghosts of her past vicarious sentiments.

Some of this nostalgia is no doubt due to outward circumstances at the time when Rinehart wrote it. In 1942, she was widowed, and the country was in the middle of World War II. The world in which Rinehart was raised had already disappeared in many ways, so, even though Hilda is only thirty-eight in this novel, she is in many ways as old as Mary Roberts Rinehart herself.

Hilda's age is rather significant in *Haunted Lady,* since she is not the only thirty-eight-year-old woman in the novel. Marian Fairbanks, whose wedding Hilda watched as a probationer, is also thirty-eight. Marian is a foil for Hilda, and her ex-husband is in a sense the husband that Hilda never had. When Marian and Frank Garrison divorced, Frank married his daughter's governess, and Hilda acted as the children's governess in "Locked Doors." When Hilda wakens Frank Garrison in his home, he mistakes her for his wife.

Hilda does not have an affair with Garrison in the novel; instead, she sees how poorly the family that she had fantasized about as a probationer has fared in the intervening years. When Hilda sees Frank Garrison again, she sees how he has aged and that he is not as prosperous as he once was. The Fairbanks house does not live up to Hilda's expectations, either—it has no "glamour" (244). The family matriarch, Mrs. Fairbanks, seems less powerful and "dominant" than Hilda remembers: "Now she was incredibly shrunken" (245).

Hilda finds the Fairbanks family very disillusioning. In looking at Marian, she finds herself thinking: "So that was what divorce did to some women! Sent them home to arbitrary old mothers, made them slip in and out of their houses, lost them their looks and their health and their zest for living." When she thinks of Frank Garrison, she realizes, "He had not looked happy, either" (254). Rather than implying that Hilda made a good choice when she decided not to marry, the novel suggests that the reason that these two people are not happy is that they should never have divorced, that the solution to the problem of their unhappiness is to get back together. It is no wonder that Hilda decides to give in to Patton's attentions.

There is one character in the novel who is reminiscent of Hilda in her early years. Carlton Fairbanks's wife, Susie, who some of the other characters feel is beneath the rest of the family, is the only character who Hilda thinks is "herself" (265). Susie also seems to have taken Hilda's place in other ways besides being comfortable with herself: she is the one who is attacked while snooping. In a sense, Hilda has lost her second profession to her. Certainly, Hilda is not comfortable with herself or either of her professions in this novel. Her hearkening back to her probationer days makes her seem inexperienced rather than experienced. At one crucial point she almost behaves like a probationer; she is ready to faint, and remembers a similar experience from her probationer days: "She had felt this way her first day in the operating room. White masks staring at her, and someone saying, 'Catch that probationer. She's going to faint.' She roused herself with an effort, forcing her eyes to focus" (299).

In *Haunted Lady*, old Mrs. Fairbanks isn't the only woman who is haunted. Hilda is haunted by the ghosts of her past and the ghost of future loneliness. She is also haunted by the culmination of her ethical questions about her work and the progressive nightmare that her detecting jobs have become. While she chooses to give in to Patton's romantic entreaties, her choice is a negative one rather than a positive one. It is no wonder that the self-confident woman of "The Buckled Bag" ends the series confused and nervous.

Works Cited

Cohn, Jan. *Improbable Fiction: The Life of Mary Roberts Rinehart*. Pittsburgh: U of Pittsburgh, 1980.

——. "Mary Roberts Rinehart." *10 Women of Mystery*. Ed. Earl F. Bargainnier. Bowling Green, OH: Bowling Green State University Popular Press, 1981. 183-220.

Davis, Robert H. *Mary Roberts Rinehart: A Sketch of the Woman and Her Work*. New York: George H. Doran, 1925.

Rinehart, Mary Roberts. "The Buckled Bag." 1914. *Miss Pinkerton: Adventures of a Nurse Detective*. New York: Rinehart, 1959. 7-54.

——. *Haunted Lady*. 1942. *Miss Pinkerton: Adventures of a Nurse Detective*. New York: Rinehart, 1959. 237-382.

——. "Locked Doors." 1914. *Miss Pinkerton: Adventures of a Nurse Detective*. New York: Rinehart, 1959. 55-92.

——. *Miss Pinkerton*. 1932. *Miss Pinkerton: Adventures of a Nurse Detective*. New York: Rinehart, 1959. 93-235.

——. *My Story: A New Edition and Seventeen New Years*. New York: Rinehart, 1948.

Uncloseting Ideology
in the Novels of Barbara Wilson

Liahna Babener

As recent critical argument has amply demonstrated, detective fiction is an ideologically encoded form, a narrative of conservative retrenchment whose objective is to undergird the dominant order, affirm bourgeois capitalism and masculine entitlement, and resecure the gender polarities upon which Western patriarchy rests.[1] The literature of detection serves a hegemonic purpose, written to "reconcile, consolidate, and obtain consent" from a readership in complicity with the fictional project of reinscribing the culture's orthodoxies (Glover 68).

In this system of signification, crime is understood not as a violation of the innocent, but rather as a symptom of the disruptions and slippages of authority that threaten to topple the power structure if they are not contained. Because society's ideological hold over its members is unstable, and because the dominant system is held together by a regime of socioeconomic and sexual repression, it is constantly susceptible to internal contradictions and abuses. Crime is the product of such systemic derangement; detection becomes the means by which these unhingings of patriarchal control are repaired.

As we know, fiction often serves culture by naturalizing its credos, making invisible its politics of domination. In this sense, the mystery form is not the revelatory vehicle it is thought to be, but rather is a discourse of concealment. Detective fiction enacts what Anne Cranny-Francis calls a "mystificatory function" by camouflaging the intrinsic oppressiveness of the social order (152). Culprits are those whose greedy excesses or transgressive behavior jeopardizes the stability of the edifice by threatening to call attention to its endemic exploitiveness; they must be individuated in such stories as miscreants or deviants in order to exempt the system itself from scrutiny. Malefactors are thus scapegoats for the culpability of the patriarchal order, while detectives become collaborators in this process of subterfuge, shielding the ideological formation from opprobrium. As a result, the law—a codification of the inequities that underpin the institutional order—escapes interrogation, and the myth of judicial neutrality is ratified. As Peter Rabinowitz has asserted, "despite the detective story's overt narrative of exposure, the formula in fact masks its violent misogyny by parading it as a form of justice" (5).

As the law's agent, the detective adumbrates the sexual politics of the genre. Underwriting a model of competitive masculinity in which power is captured and held by excoriating and suppressing the feminine, conventional detective stories are structured around male triumph over the distractions of desire and the threat of otherness. The detective is recruited to shore up gender structures that tend to crumble continually under the weight of their vulnerability to such forces and their own abusive proclivities. Teresa Ebert argues forcefully that crime fictions are "narratives of crisis in patriarchy" (6) wherein

the detective . . . enforces the Law-of-the-Father (through violence if necessary) ensuring that individuals line up on the side of the phallic divide signaled by their anatomy, and he preserves and secures the system of privilege, labor, and exploitation based on gender, resolving its contradictions and restoring its . . . legitimacy. (8)

It becomes the drive of such fiction, then, to redeem and validate the ideology of masculinity, interpellating readers into that conceptual framework through a series of textual maneuvers designed to consecrate sexual difference. The detective, as enforcer of the hegemonic system, proclaims and acts out his sexual identity by employing investigative tactics understood as masculine modes of behavior. He uses a scopic gaze to control by the act of looking the objects of his probe, a logocentric logic to order reality in amenable ways, and a punitive violence to valorize his manhood—all aids of detection that serve as instruments to conscript male readers into a position of surrogacy in this project; female readers are barred access to the discourse, or must engage in a kind of mental transvestism to take pleasure in it.[2]

In the textual world of detection, women must be essentialized into Woman, rendered erotically lethal, vilified, and defeated, a task made simpler by what in Lacan's terms is woman's confinement outside the pale of language where she is kept mute and impotent, and subject to malicious construction by masculine speech. Most classic examples of the hard-boiled genre feature women characters whose noncompliant behavior—owning their own desire and acting upon it, against patriarchal strictures—is seen as menacing to the insecure male psyche and potentially catastrophic to the social scheme constituted around it; not surprisingly, the imperative of such fiction is to subdue female agency and desire. The investigator's assignment is to apprehend the sexed woman and disenfranchise her, thus quashing the castration threat she embodies. Typically, these texts end with her demise through detention or death, a disposition warranted by, indeed mandated by, patriarchal law.

Classic detection, then, is rooted in a deep-seated fear of the feminine, which is seen as a dissident force intent upon unfixing the gender codes that hold the dominant culture in position. More broadly, the project of traditional detective fiction is to "veil and contain sexual ambiguity" in Maggie Humm's words (238), pacifying a ubiquitous homophobic anxiety and imposing the *lex non scripta* of heteronormativity that is a cornerstone of the patriarchal construct. Adrienne Rich and Monique Wittig provide vigorous statements of the ways in which "sex is naturalized as the straight mind: taken for granted and pervasively unsaid, heterosexuality is a 'core of nature' in all of the texts of culture . . . a regime of power and violence on which a broad network of oppressive social arrangements depends" (Hennessy 970).

Popular fictions become the implements by which the "unsaid" dogmas of culture are articulated and indoctrinated, and the literature of detection assumes this function with avidity. As David Glover points out,

In the thriller male agency is staged as self-determined, active, brutal, while at the same time it is undercut by a profound sense of homosocial unease. The two are indissolubly linked for, given the premium placed upon the endurance and integrity of the male body as the condition of narrative movement, homosexuality represents the ultimate terror. . . . Homosexuality remains unfinished business for the thriller's male order and has almost invariably been depicted in uncompromisingly bleak and contemptuous terms. (77-78)

Hence, the genre bears the burden of reauthorizing male sexual dominance by occulting the homoerotic. In a culture where the fragile masculine ego feels itself perennially under siege by challenges to the established sexual hierarchies, the need to reinvest detective heroes with phallic prerogative is all the more emphatic.

This may be one perspective from which to read much contemporary literature featuring hard-boiled women investigators. While it is clearly the case that novels by writers such as Sue Grafton, Marcia Muller, Sara Paretsky, Liza Cody, and others, all of which foreground female operatives and reflect a feminist sensibility, represent attempts to appropriate and reconceptualize the genre, and while they do claim a fiercely committed readership of women, it is not necessarily the case that these fictions work successfully to dismantle patriarchal ideologies or undercut the hegemony of heterosexuality.[3] It might be argued that, in fact, such texts ultimately reinforce the gender divide, in spite of the ways in which they may be thought to empower women readers. Teresa Ebert has contended that these female sleuths should be read as deputy henchmen for patriarchy, since the disciplinary practice of detection itself is irremediably invested with phallic authority:

In mainstream women detective novels, the woman detective functions as an agent of patriarchy, and if she is a feminist she often does so in spite of herself and her politics. Her detecting ends up restoring patriarchal order and containing its contradictions. This is not to say that some women detectives do not engage in significant criticisms of patriarchal institutions. . . . [Yet] the main issue of such criticism . . . is women's lack of power *within* patriarchy. But such an agenda is in many ways complicit with and supplementary to patriarchy: it does not propose to overthrow the patriarchal regime; rather, it merely seeks a place for women *within* that regime. The narrative thus articulates a "patriarchal feminism." (14-15)

The effect of such ideological and discursive constraints may be to make detection "an unsuitable job for a feminist," as Kathleen Klein has suggested, since "no woman detective escapes the prospect of assisting in her own or other women's oppression. . . . [She is] bound to that system which [she] may despise but cannot escape" (*Woman Detective* 201). As most of these narratives situate themselves in the bourgeois milieu, their contestatory power is already compromised. Detectives like Sharon McCone and Kinsey Millhone may be seen to be, in effect, safeguarding "heterosexual middle class white males and their female slaves" (Forrest 109-10). Even those like V.I. Warshawski, products of working-class backgrounds who act as self-aware advocates of society's dispossessed, end up negotiating the cultural resistances represented by their clientele and thus capitulating to the strategies of domination enforced by the heteropatriarchy.

The task of disrupting gendered discourse has proved to be a formidable one, and many theorists argue that, because the phallocentric semantic system circumscribes the possibilities of meaning, there can be no escape from it. Nonetheless, authors continue to find strategies to rewrite the role of gender in culture, breaching the conventions of detective fiction to create a feminist counter-narrative. To do so means, as Klein has put it, to "challenge the genre at both its surface and core" ("Habeas" 9), reconfiguring its patterns of utterance, defining anew the structures of human relationships that constitute the social order, probing the endemic criminality of patriarchy, and ungendering subjectivity; the genre must be deployed to contravene rather than confirm fictional tradition, the author's stance made expressly oppositional, and the reading position constructed as feminist.[4]

While feminist mystery writers have, with varying degrees of success, attempted such ideological interventions, the impediments, especially to the project of disassembling the architectonics of gender, are manifold, since "the fixed structure of detective fiction will always pull back towards a hierarchical, establishment world and a faith in traditional authority" (Coward and Semple 49). To evacuate received categories of gender requires a more drastic act of textual infringement. Writing from a position outside the heterosexual binary, a number of lesbian authors have demonstrated the adversarial power of narratives devoted to decoding and reconstituting the sociosymbolic system, using the literature of detection to effect a radical reconceptualization of the categories of gender. Because the homoerotic has been culturally suppressed, and lesbianism in particular written out of phallocentric language, lesbian identity may be the very vantage point from which a profitable cultural critique can take place; in marginality is power. Theorized, as Wittig explains, as "not-woman" (since "woman" is defined only in subaltern relation to "man" in hegemonic discourse), the lesbian exists outside of the imbalanced bipolarities that frame culture (13). It is here, in an independent discursive terrain, that narrative reinvention can occur, yielding a re-visioned detective literature and generating "a legitimating, cleansing, recuperative version of lesbian erotic life" (Yorke 30).

The novels of Barbara Wilson featuring lesbian investigator Pam Nilson come closest, in my view, to achieving both the deconstruction of the genre and the affirmation of same-sex desire as an alternative cultural formulation.[5] In *Murder in the Collective* (1984), *Sisters of the Road* (1986), and *The Dog Collar Murders* (1989), Wilson meshes these objectives, constructing lesbian experience and collectivity as subversive counterpoints to patriarchal structures. All three novels both reiterate and interrogate the fictional conventions of detection, enabling a pointed critique of the genre and its political ideologies, while offering a positive refiguration of the human community that ameliorates the cultural evils as diagnosed. Pam remodels the discipline of detection, converting it from agency on behalf of the state to a form of trespass against the phallocratic regime. In evolving her own lesbian subjectivity, she challenges notions of heterosexual autonomy imbedded in standard constructions of the detective, proffering a more complex vision of experience and inviting a more compelling identificatory posture for women readers.[6]

If, as Rachel DuPlessis has noted, narrative structure is "the place where ideology is coiled," Wilson invents discourse that uncurls itself, freeing the serpent from the text (5). Her fiction refuses the patternings of standard masculine scripts with their obdurate linearity, sequential plotting, and unrelenting push toward apogee and closure—features usually thought quintessential to the inductive methodology and apocalyptic function of detection. Gone too is the virile vocality that usually characterizes hard-boiled mysteries, a kind of masculine "overinsistence which comes close to parody at times—defensive, brutalizing and territorial" (Bromley 106), and grounded in sexual paranoia. Wilson's novels violate this paradigm, affording a feminist model of articulation. The linguistic and structural strategies are those associated with women's writing: interrupted momentum and retarded denouement, polyvocal narration and dialogic speech, and idioms drawn from female worlds of experience.

All three novels are told from the first-person point of view, a commonplace in the "tough" school of detective fiction. But Wilson uses the personal mode to displace rather than replay verbal tradition. In narrating her own stories, Pam positions herself—a woman, a lesbian, an iconoclast—as authorizing agent of the diegesis, freeing it from standard ideological duty to define manhood and uphold patriarchal dicta. Her accounts, which interfuse the processes of investigation and identity formation, abjure the euphemistic style that functions to hide and deny desire in male texts; rather, the pursuit of meaning that detection entails is reenacted in her endeavor to seek and live out a lesbian sexuality. It might also be argued that Wilson foregrounds Pam's erotic awakening tactically in order to countermand the formulaic dictum "that it is women's transgressive sexuality that is 'the problem'—the trigger of social disturbance and violence" (Kaplan 19). Here, the antithesis is the case: lesbian sexuality is a redemptive force.

In *Murder in the Collective,* the first of the series, Pam's quest to identify the killer of Jeremy Plaice is inseparably bound up in her devolving homosexual profile. In untangling the knot of Jeremy's secret history, Pam develops an ability to read the nuances of relationships and sort out disparities of sexual power which she comes to apply her own life. It turns out that Jeremy is a CIA agent and paid informant of the dictatorial Philippines government posing as a leftist activist; he is also revealed to be the husband of Zee, a member of Pam's publications collective who has fled the Philippines and is now engaged in anti-Marcos politics. Discerning the covert terrorism that Jeremy has practiced on those whose cultural subordination he could exploit as a government operative and a privileged white man (Filipino dissidents risking exposure and death for their activities; a lesbian with a history of abuse at the hands of men, whom he rapes; his current lover who is misled by his revolutionary pretense; and especially his wife, who is effectively coerced into marrying him to achieve political sanctuary), Pam makes the crucial connection between imperialism and hetero-sexuality, recognizing the oppressive power of both institutions. This insight gives impetus to her own homoerotic odyssey; at the time of the investigation, she is coming to recognize and ultimately celebrate her attraction to other women.

Pam's evolutionary coming out, a process of fits and starts, backtracking then advancing, finding joyous but impermanent consummation in lover Hadley Harper, is signaled textually by her fragmented utterances of desire ("I wasn't a lesbian, but I was sort of interested, but I didn't know, but I sort of wanted to find out, but I couldn't be sure, but I really liked her, but maybe just as a friend" [*Collective* 101]) and figuratively reprised in her halting reconnaissance of Jeremy's death. Too, her new lesbian status implements her detection in unanticipated ways. As Marilyn Frye has maintained, the cultural erasure that lesbians suffer leaves them outside the conceptual scheme, "unreal" in a sense, since "to be real is to be visible to the king," and "lesbians are not named in the lexicon of the King's English" (155). Invisibility grants her unpublicized entry into the circles of power where the solution to the mystery resides, and it enhances her empathy with social victimization.

The ending pages of *Murder in the Collective* underscore the narrative integration of lesbian self-discovery and detection, as Pam and Hadley retrace the investigation and playfully envision a sleuthing partnership called "Amazons, Inc." (180). The concluding section also refuses conventional textual gratification, displaying the alienation between the two women that has blunted their romance, and reminding readers of the analytical disjunctions that have impeded the case—Pam's blindness to Zee's vengeful hatred, for example, and her facile racial liberalism which has prompted her to exonerate uncritically one of the suspects because she is African-American. In the scene where the climactic disclosure would occur had this been a classical mystery, Pam's obtuseness and prejudices are reprimanded by one of her colleagues who accuses her of playing at espionage when women's lives are at stake, spoiling the dramatic exposé Pam had planned. And even at this moment, Pam does not know for certain who the killer is; later, when Zee is unmasked, her fate is left uncertain.

This thwarted denouement, with its imbedded critique of detection and mocking deflation of Pam, works as a subversive device, signaling

Wilson's departure from the masculine coda prescribing a singular arbiter of textual signification a la Sherlock Holmes or Philip Marlowe. The novel, in keeping with its title, offers an aggregate model of investigation, where the company of participants (the members of the print collective) merge to unriddle the mystery. The detection process, and thus the construction of meaning, is shared, reflecting a multiplicity of voices that deters the totalizing drive of patriarchal fictions.

Too, the foundational opposition between detective and wrongdoer that serves a hegemonic function in traditional crime literature is discarded here, not merely because the conclave of detectives is also the conclave of suspects (everyone is implicated in the killing of Jeremy), but also because, in the end, Zee is championed for having eradicated a phallic punisher. It is not insignificant that Pam and her repertory of fellow operatives decide to shield Zee from police intelligence, a seditious act done in the service of a feminist design to disempower the law. The law, after all, had sanctioned Jeremy's victimizing behavior as a CIA agent and his abuses as a man. By protecting Zee from discovery and prosecution, Pam and her cohorts enact a resistance that marks the text's expressly inimical stance against the dominant system, underscoring the point that it is the system itself that is the malefactor; Zee's "crime" is reconfigured as a heroic act.

The female collaboration that evolves to find and then vindicate Jeremy's killer represents more than a revisioned concept of detection and extends beyond feminist insurrection. Pam's collective stands for a radical reconceptualization of the societal norms that are now organized into the heterosexual pairings and nuclear families of patriarchy, an alternative model of human relatedness "illustrating the importance of female strength through community in opposition to male strength through individual heroism" (Irons 129). The group values the mutual well-being of its members over the autonomy of any one, positing an idea of inter-connectedness, supportiveness, and love that can only flourish in a domain uncontaminated by heterosexism. (This is, of course, one reason why Jeremy, a partner in the collective at the outset of the novel, must be removed.)

Wilson charts the strivings of the collective to form itself around such principles and depicts Pam's own endeavor to negotiate her complex involvements with its members in order to fit within such a frame. She must come to terms with June, a working-class woman who faults Pam's middle-class white blinders; her twin sister Penny, to whom she is bound in familial history but whose heterosexuality may present a barrier to their continued closeness; Ray, Pam's former lover, who is now involved with her sister, thus standing as a kind of double throwback to Pam's prior self; Elena, whose proposal to merge with a lesbian printing cooperative sets the parallel events of the story—the inquiry into Jeremy's death and Pam's sexual awakening—into motion; and Zee, whom Pam both accuses and excuses. In spotlighting the group's process of interpersonal mediation, Wilson, as Maureen Reddy has suggested, "places concern for relationships ahead of such abstractions as order and justice" ("Feminist" 183), affirming a social pattern based on ministrations to need rather than obedience to regulations. The collective is an egalitarian rather than a vertical structure—a direct challenge to patriarchal formations.

Wilson carries the idea of a counter-ideology further in her depiction of the lesbian community that Pam is drawn to. Fully cognizant of the diverse patterns and complex arrangements born of female same-sex desire, Wilson portrays lesbian life in all its rich versatility. Gay characters in the novel reflect a range of demeanors and behaviors: Fran is "a Queen Victoria of dykedom" (*Collective* 26)— imperious, earthy, vibrant; Elena is a refugee from an oppressive marriage, hardened by hurt; Hadley is an urban sophisticate whose intense but abbreviated affairs with a succession of women rankle Pam, herself more inclined to a monogamous kind of partnership. In spite of the differing models of homosexuality these characters afford, they have in common a renunciation of the oppressions of heterosexism and an abiding commitment to a way of life shaped by female love. Wilson's choice to build her fiction around and articulate what Teresa de Lauretis calls "another way of thinking the sexual" (iii), a "woman-woman bond as between one subject and another subject" (Yorke 33) as opposed to the gendered hierarchy of heterosexual coupling, constitutes the author's most significant challenge to the dogmas of traditional popular literature.

Sisters of the Road expands upon the idea of finding other ways of "thinking the sexual," exploring as it does the troubling libidinal politics of adolescent prostitution, child sexual abuse, and rape, while simultaneously presenting the evolving story of Pam Nilson's emotional maturation as a lesbian. Pam has stumbled into the aftermath of a violent assault upon Rosalie, a young streetwalker; the girl dies, and her teenaged companion, Trish, who holds the key to the killer's identity—and who invites Pam's altruism as a social sufferer—has run away from Pam's protective care. In searching for her charge, Pam must piece together the recurrent pattern of abuse and escape that has driven the girl to the streets, and find a way to interrupt it. The novel builds upon ideas of female communalism and safekeeping advanced in *Collective,* and repeats the transgressive textual strategies of the first book to advance Wilson's mission of jettisoning formula fiction's patriarchal support system.

Central to the critique of cultural misogyny is Wilson's complex rendering of the domain of prostitution. While it may be a staple of feminist thought that prostitution is an exploitive institution that engraves women's position in patriarchy as commodities of male exchange, Wilson subjects this contention to sustained interrogation in the story, which no less unabashedly dramatizes the squalor and brutality of sex for hire. Pam is spared no illusions as she journeys into this sordid world to find Trish. Her exposure to the hardened victims of social dislocation—youthful runaways, drug addicts, battery victims, socio-paths, pimps, and prostitutes—opens her eyes to the vile excesses of bourgeois patriarchy. A social worker tutors her in seamy realities of street life:

A lot of the girls on the street aren't really into prostitution in a big way. They come downtown, running from their parents, looking for drugs and company— and after a few days, when they're hungry and cold and out of cash, one of their new friends tells them where it's at, how easy it is to get into the car with one of the men cruising by. You suck or jerk him off while he drives around the block and there's your twenty bucks. No big deal. (Sisters 57)

Pam may not be surprised at this odious image of anonymous male lust, but she is unprepared for the dazed nonchalance of the child whores she meets, who seem resigned to a life of systematic usage and degradation.

Pam's first judgments, however, are not allowed to stand uncritically; they are complicated and tested by an internal textual dialogue that extends the multivocal articulation and group detection in *Collective*. Wilson organizes the narrative as an ongoing debate among the women who participate in the sex industry, serve as advocates for its victims, or witness its effects. As Kathleen Klein has observed, the "heteroglossic arguments" of the text deconstruct the genre's standard "oppositional discourse of right and wrong" ("Habeas" 13), disallowing a reductive vision of women's lives, even under conditions of severe ill-usage.

Pam hears the prostitutes' apologia from Janis Glover, a feminist lawyer whom she meets in the course of her investigation:

You can't just go around feeling sorry for them and thinking they got a raw deal in life. A lot of them make more money than I do and would be perfectly satisfied with life if the cops didn't harass them. . . . Most prostitutes I've met feel like they're the ones in control, using men to get back what's owing to them economically. Hell if they care about being poor and pure! (*Sisters* 128)

The discussion continues when Pam meets Dawn Jacobs, a thirtyish call girl who turned to hooking when her divorce left her unable to support her children. She defends her occupation: "it's easy work and I've got my regular customers, had some of them for years" (145). Bonnie, another prostitute, points out, "What's so different about what I'm doing and what you did when you were married? You had to get down on your hands and knees to get any money out of Alan, you slept with him when you didn't feel like it just to keep him happy so's he'd keep supporting you—and he didn't even do that!" (145).

Pam is forced to acknowledge her own ambivalence about the subject, pondering the way harlots have been culturally mythologized both as beguiling sirens and "diseased hags" (134). She is persuaded in some respects by the mutinous spirit of these women, but unable to forswear her deeper conviction that hired sex is a form of female enslavement. Later, discovering that Trish had fled a dysfunctional home and sexual molestation by her father, Pam must contextualize the girl's life of prostitution, recognizing that in an ironic way it had represented a sanctuary to her from the more insidious violations of incest and parental neglect.

As a feminist fictional maneuver, the dialogism of the narrative here works to subvert standard textual practice, impeding the progress of the plot (much of the novel's central section is devoted to this sustained debate about the justifications for and deleterious consequences of prostitution), and abnegating the kind of singularized meaning that crime fiction usually aspires to. Yet the voices in the debate coalesce as expressions of womanly rage and vindication. In spite of its disruptive design as a multivocal narrative, in another sense the story accomplishes its emotional sway over women readers as well as its structural cohesiveness through the deeper commonality of the positions advanced by the various speakers. Each vents indignation at the violations against women perpetuated by a misogynist system, under whose auspices such misconduct is sanitized and sanctified. As Maureen Reddy has noted, "most of the crimes investigated in lesbian feminist crime fiction are committed by men against women as a way of forcing women's obedience to patriarchal order" (*Sisters in Crime* 131).

As we saw in *Collective,* Wilson foregrounds instances of female oppression in order to position the text counteractively against them. In *Sisters,* the abuse is more vicious and hate filled, while the social acquittal of those responsible is more indefeasible. Trish's father, for example, who had molested her when she was barely five years old, has escaped liability for his offense: "I came to Portland and started over. I found Jesus—and Judy" (*Sisters* 140). Propped up by born-again

Christianity and a servile wife, both appliances of male power, Margolin is made to stand for the intrinsic (and literal) turpitude of the Law-of-the-Father.

A yet more salient illustration of this point is the portrayal of Wayne Hemmings, Trish's stepbrother, who is also the one who turned her on to drugs, used her sexually and bartered her to his friends, and pressed her into prostitution. Hemmings, it turns out, had also been Rosalie's pimp; he had slain her, Pam discovers, in a fit of pique when he learned of the girl's plan to get herself and Trish off the streets and break free of his domination. Wayne's murderous fury is set in motion by his sense of being disinherited by the girls' show of independence. Convinced that the right to own and abuse women is his masculine birthright—a prerogative historically codified in law—Wayne sets himself up as patriarchal punisher: "Yeah, I killed Rosalie. You want to know why? The bitch . . . said she and Trish should get a piece of the action. Like Trish belonged to her or something, the fucking nigger whore. Trish belongs to *me*" (193).

Wayne's outrage is amplified by his racist aversion, and further by his homophobic repugnance of Rosalie's lesbianism. (Wayne's homophobia is augmented by his deep anxiety about his own sexual propensities: he had started in the sex business as a prostitute serving male clients himself. He is quick to assert that he's not gay, but the reader picks up the self-loathing that underlies his rage.) In the confrontation where Pam accuses Wayne, the whole putrefying slew of masculine resentment gushes out and threatens to engulf her. Wayne enacts the age-old male vengeance against Pam—as woman, homosexual, and enemy Other—by raping her. Significantly, when the police arrive following the rape, they spend their energies preventing Pam's friend June from striking her violator rather than ministering to the victim, reminding readers again of the ways in which the law colludes in women's brutalization.

Wilson's feminist textual strategies are particularly in evidence in this scene. The narration is framed around Pam's reactions during and after the event—her horror, pain, and vulnerability—enhancing womanly empathy with Pam's torment while denying readers verbal access to the rapist's point of view. By granting graphic textual license to the sufferer and eclipsing the perpetrator's gratification, Wilson reverses the generic practice that eroticizes sexual violence. As Sally Munt has written, "*Sisters of the Road* sets out to destroy some of the vicariousness of crime fiction—this is no comfortable fantasy" (105). The novel thus shares the revisionist objectives that Laura Mulvey identifies as the task of feminist analysis: the eradication of pleasure, insofar as pleasure is understood to be male voyeuristic thralldom. Instead, the textual moment in this final phase of the novel that inspires pleasure for female readers is the poignant one that shows Trish, now rising from her former wretchedness, comforting Pam, offering sisterly consolation for her sorrow and a hope for psychic deliverance that can only come from one who has endured the same plight.

Acting throughout the text as another counterforce to the exploitations·of the heteropatriarchy is the lesbian feminist support network that facilitates Pam's efforts to rescue Trish. Set against the inefficacy and connivance of masculinist law enforcement, the system of women helping women supplants officialdom as the agent of female justice. Pam's friend Carole helps her secure crucial evidence in the case; Beth, a counselor for juvenile victims, helps her locate Janis, who in turn educates her about the urban underworld of hired sex. It is through their collaborative efforts that Trish is found and Rosalie's murderer apprehended.

Though her membership in the lesbian continuum has now been established, Pam's carnal life is on hold during the course of the novel. In fact, in the way that her fiction consciously disobeys formulaic expectations, Wilson subverts the progress of love in Pam's life. *Collective* ends with Pam and Hadley separating; in a gesture meant to divest Pam of a falsely exotic image of her, Hadley removes her contact lenses and reveals a plainer natural face. Wilson employs the scene sportively, to demystify the sexual idealization that readers might anticipate in a popular genre, and stresses Pam's status as a woman in romantic transition. Again in *Sisters,* Pam's pursuit of a lover is made awkwardly comic, as she makes advances to a disinterested Carole. By obstructing these amorous unions, Wilson reinforces her broader stratagem of discursive interruption, and eschews a simplistic or utopian rendering of lesbian pairing.

The Dog Collar Murders returns to the thematics of lesbian experience, this time subjecting not only romantic liaisons among women but the whole concept of a mutually supportive and ideologically cohesive lesbian community to a sharply scrutinizing lens. Pam's involvement with Hadley undergoes renegotiation for the duration of the story. In the end, the two invent a relational structure that enables their closeness but mitigates against a constrictive kind of coupling. Having lived together as lovers, they now adopt a model of parallel but separate households, two residences in a building they own jointly. The arrangement is deliberately idiosyncratic, meant to resist standard heterosexual domestic formations—like the marriage that Pam's twin, Penny, has just contracted—and to demonstrate how "lesbian desire transgresses the boundaries of stories that are imaginable in dominant fictions" (Woodward 842).

More problematical is the way the novel calls into question the notion of lesbian communalism presented in the prior two books. The mystery revolves around Pam's quest to find the killer of Loie Marsh, a feminist antipornography lobbyist murdered just after her speech before a national conference on sexuality that Pam is attending. The victim has been asphyxiated by a dog collar, a pointed reference to the controversial accoutrements of erotica used in pornography to signal the submissive position in sadomasochistic activity. Marsh's campaign has targeted all purveyors of pornographic images, both gay and straight, whom she sees as perpetrators of social crimes against women. Her denunciation has angered practitioners of lesbian sadomasochism, who consider her position to be censorial, unmindful of the diversities of female sexuality. A second homicide—or femicide—of one Marsh's critics, a defender of lesbian pornography who is dispatched by the same method, complicates the investigation and highlights the ambiguity of the sexual questions at stake in the deliberations.

As commentators have observed, the debate over these topics in *Dog Collar Murders* dominates the narrative, emphasizing Wilson's characteristically polysemic narration.[7] Pam's personal attitudes about pornography, exhibitionism, bondage, and other variant sexual activities are unstable to start with, and jostled all the more by the nuanced arguments of a range of speakers on every side of these issues. She listens not merely to formal advocacy by conference presenters, but to the impassioned yet radically divergent viewpoints of her friends, all of whom profess a feminist disposition, in a simultaneous attempt to shape her own sexual philosophy and to unearth a murderer.

Pam's perplexity is more than intellectual as she is both stimulated and offended by the erotic displays she witnesses by the in-your-face contingent of lesbian activists. A tour of the porno marketplace leaves her bewildered:

After about thirty minutes my curiosity had turned from lust to queasiness to a sad feeling that human beings had been created for another purpose than to loll about with their tongues sticking out, having their various orifices and protuberances photographed and sold for great sums of money. I didn't know what that purpose was . . . but it had to be different from this. (*Dog Collar Murders* 59)

The format of the text accentuates its concern with larger unresolvable questions about the nature of desire, and makes visible Wilson's commitment to a multivocal discourse, unsettling not merely patriarchal pronouncements about sexual matters but also the idea of lesbian solidarity that Wilson has herself affirmed. Hence, the fictional subversion extends to her own practices. This idea is playfully reiterated at the end of the novel when Pam, exhausted from contemplating the varied voices of the debate on pornography, urges a "moratorium" on the discussion: "I think I'm kind of talked out for awhile," she tells a friend, who counters, "What kind of feminist are you? . . .You can't be talked-*out*!" (203).

Notwithstanding the novel's internal query of feminist precepts, its thrust is to challenge hegemonic values through the process of detection. The murderer, it turns out, is a spokeswoman for the Christian right who, along with her husband and a network of like-minded minions, is engaged in "pro-family" politics and at the helm of a crusade to cleanse the airwaves. Couching a retrograde social agenda in moderate language and reasoned argument, Sonya Gustafson masquerades as a humanitarian whose mission is to protect people from baneful influences, winning the public credibility that shields her from political scrutiny. Pam's investigation reveals the heteropatriarchal ideology behind Sonya's program ("putting homosexuals in concentration camps . . . and making abortion and contraception illegal" [49]), thus properly separating Sonya's impugnment of pornography (rooted in the kind of sexual paranoia about female desire that results in repression) from the opposition of feminists, who protest its injurious effects upon women.

The revelation that Sonya and her husband had participated years ago in the making of amateur sex movies—a fact which of course invests her current antagonism with an element of hypocrisy—and are now killing those with knowledge of their past indiscretions, suggests the desperation of the phallic regime to protect its power; it also points up the ways women, as wives in traditional marriages, are drafted into the cause of containing the excesses of patriarchy. The fact that Loie Marsh had once been married to David Gustafson augments the book's argument that traditional ideologies harness women's insecurities, encouraging then exploiting a sexual rivalry over men. To advance this notion is not, however, to reprise the standard dogma of female jealousy and embitterment. Wilson, rather, allows empathy for Sonya whose plight is the result of having bought into the phallocentric system, the true perpetrator. It was David Gustafson who was instrumental in making those damaging pornographic films, and he who played the women in his life off against each other to exert sexual control. This recognition implements the novel's critique of male domination and reinforces the virtues of the lesbian community which, though subjected to intense examination, is shown to be modeled on principles other than the "power-imbued discourse of heterosexual relations" (Palmer 22).

Wilson, then, uses the detective format as a tool to break conventional narrative codes, undermining the system of heteronormativity enforced through traditional literary formulas and replacing it with a resistant culture, lesbian and feminist. Ultimately, these novels work on several levels to enfranchise readers: unraveling generic paradigms, denaturalizing heterosexist credos, recentering marginal figures, and celebrating—though not uncritically and not unmindful of differences—the egalitarian tenets and carnal joys of lesbian life. As Sally Munt has suggested, "the reader reads to discover 'herself,' but also to reconstruct 'herself' as a woman empowered and centered. The novels offer a fantasy of control, and so radically invert the real relations of her oppression" (111). While it may not be possible to capsize patriarchy, Wilson demonstrates that it is possible to destablilize the lexical system upon which it rests.

Notes

1. For substantial discussions of the ways in which traditional detective fiction, particularly the hard-boiled subgenre, inscribes social conservatism and reinforces standard gender norms, see especially Bromley, Cranny-Francis, Coward and Semple, Ebert, Glover, Humm, Irons, Kaplan, Klein (*Woman Detective* and "Habeas"), Knight (*Form and Ideology* and "Radical Thrillers"), Munt, Palmer, Pykett, Reddy (*Sisters in Crime* and "Feminist"), and B. Ruby Rich.

2. See Mary Anne Doane's and Laura Mulvey's work on female spectatorship in the cinema for a full discussion of female transvestism.

3. A compelling argument about the empowerment of Sue Grafton's female readership is made by Priscilla L. Walton in this volume.

4. See Anne Cranny-Francis on the notion of constructing a feminist reading position, particularly the Introduction (1-28) and the chapter on "Feminist Detective Fiction" (143-76).

5. Among the many writers employing lesbian detectives whose work achieves similar ends are: M.F. Beal, Lauren Wright Douglas, Sarah Dreher, Ellen Hart, Katherine Forrest (discussed in this collection), Vicki P. McConnell, Rebecca O'Rourke, Sarah Schulman, and Mary Wings.

6. It is important to stress that lesbian experience and identity are emphatically various. Whether lesbian selfhood is found or fashioned, essential or evolves, is a matter of rigorous debate among gay theorists. For a thorough discussion of these issues, see Shane Phelan, Judith Butler, Lisa M. Walker, and Valerie Traub.

7. See especially Reddy ("Feminist") and Klein ("Habeas").

Works Cited

Bromley, Roger. "Rewriting the Masculine Script: The Novels of Joseph Hansen." *Gender, Genre and Narrative Pleasure.* Ed. Derek Longhurst. London: Unwin Hyman, 1989. 102-17.

Butler, Judith. "Imitation and Gender Insubordination." *The Lesbian and Gay Studies Reader.* Ed. Henry Abelove, Michele Aina Barale, and David M. Halperin. New York and London: Routledge, 1993. 307-20.

Coward, Rosalind, and Linda Semple. "Tracking Down the Past: Women and Detective Fiction." *From My Guy to Sci Fi: Genre and Women's Writing in the Postmodern World.* Ed. Helen Carr. London: Pandora, 1989. 39-57.

Cranny-Francis, Anne. *Feminist Fiction: Feminist Uses of Generic Fiction.* New York: St. Martin's, 1990.

De Lauretis, Teresa. "Introduction." *Differences* 3.2 (1991): iii-xviii.

DuPlessis, Rachel Blau. *Writing Beyond the Ending: Narrative Strategies of Twentieth-Century Women Writers.* Bloomington: Indiana UP, 1985.

Doane, Mary Ann. *The Desire to Desire: The Woman's Film of the 1940's.* Bloomington and Indianapolis: Indiana UP, 1987.

Ebert, Teresa L. "Detecting the Phallus: Authority, Ideology, and the Production of Patriarchal Agents in Detective Fiction." *Rethinking Marxism* 5.3 (Fall 1992): 6-28.

Frye, Marilyn. *The Politics of Reality: Essays in Feminist Theory.* Trumansburg, NY: Crossing, 1983.

Forrest, Katherine. *Murder at the Nightwood Bar.* Tallahassee: Naiad, 1989.

Glover, David. "The Stuff That Dreams Are Made of: Masculinity, Femininity and the Thriller." *Gender, Genre and Narrative Pleasure.* Ed. Derek Longhurst. London: Unwin Hyman, 1989. 67-83.

Hennessy, Rosemary. "Queer Theory: A Review of the *differences* Special Issue and Wittig's *The Straight Mind.*" *Signs* 18.4 (Summer 1993): 964-73.

Humm, Maggie. "Feminist Detective Fiction." *Twentieth Century Suspense: The Thriller Comes of Age.* Ed. Clive Bloom. New York: St. Martin's, 1990. 237-54.

Irons, Glenwood. "New Woman Detectives: G is for Gender-Bending." *Gender, Language and Myth: Essays on Popular Narrative.* Ed. Glenwood Irons. Toronto: U of Toronto P, 1992. 127-41.

Kaplan, Cora. "An Unsuitable Genre for a Feminist?" *Women's Review* 8 (June 1986): 18-19.

Klein, Kathleen. "Habeas Corpus: Feminism and Detective Fiction." *The New Women Detectives.* Ed. Glenwood Irons. Toronto: U of Toronto P. Forthcoming.

——. *The Woman Detective: Gender and Genre*. Urbana and Chicago: U of Illinois P, 1988.

Knight, Stephen. *Form and Ideology in Crime Fiction*. Bloomington: Indiana UP, 1980.

——. "Radical Thrillers." *Watching the Detectives: Essays on Crime Fiction*. Ed. Ian A. Bell and Graham Daldry. New York: St. Martin's, 1990: 172-87.

Mulvey, Laura. "Visual Pleasure and Narrative Cinema." *Screen* 16.3 (Autumn 1975): 6-18.

Munt, Sally. "The Inverstigators: Lesbian Crime Fiction." *Sweet Dreams: Sexuality, Gender and Popular Fiction*. Ed. Susannah Radstone. London: Laurence and Wishart, 1988. 91-119.

Palmer, Paulina. "The Lesbian Feminist Thriller and Detective Novel." *What Lesbians Do in Books*. Ed. Elaine Hobby and Chris White. London: Women's Press, 1991. 9-27.

Phelan, Shane. "(Be)Coming Out: Lesbian Identity and Politics." *Signs* 18.4 (Summer 1993): 765-90.

Pykett, Lyn. "Investigating Women: The Female Sleuth after Feminism." *Watching the Detectives: Essays on Crime Fiction*. Ed. Ian A. Bell and Graham Daldry. New York: St. Martin's, 1990. 48-67.

Rabinowitz, Peter J. "'Reader, I Blew Him Away': Convention and Transgression in Sue Grafton." *Famous Last Words: Changes in Gender & Narrative Closure*. Ed. Alison Booth. Charlottesville, VA: U of Virginia P, 1993. 326-46.

Reddy, Maureen T. "The Feminist Counter-Tradition in Crime: Cross, Grafton, Paretsky, and Wilson." *The Cunning Craft: Original Essays on Detective Fiction and Contemporary Literary Theory*. Ed. Ronald G. Walker and June M. Frazer. Macomb, IL: Essays in Literature, 1990. 174-87.

——. *Sisters in Crime: Feminism and the Crime Novel*. New York: Continuum, 1988.

Rich, Adrienne. "Compulsory Heterosexuality and Lesbian Existence." *Signs* 5.4 (Summer 1980): 631-60.

Rich, B. Ruby. "The Lady Dicks: Genre Benders Take the Case." *Voice Literary Supplement* June 1989: 24-27.

Traub, Valerie. "The Ambiguities of 'Lesbian' Viewing Pleasure: The (Dis)articulations of *Black Widow*." *Body Guards: The Cultural Politics of Gender Ambiguity*. Ed. Julia Epstein and Kristina Straub. New York and London: Routledge, 1991. 305-28.

Walker, Lisa M. "How to Recognize a Lesbian: The Cultural Politics of Looking Like What You Are." *Signs* 18.4 (Summer 1993): 866-90.

Wilson, Barbara. *The Dog Collar Murders*. Seattle: Seal, 1989.

——. *Murder in the Collective*. Seattle: Seal, 1984.

——. *Sisters of the Road*. Seattle, WA: Seal, 1986.

Wittig, Monique. *The Straight Mind and Other Essays*. Boston: Beacon, 1992.

Woodward, Carlyn. "'My Heart So Wrapt': Lesbian Disruptions in Eighteenth-Century British Fiction." *Signs* 18.4 (Summer 1993): 838-65.

Yorke, Liz. "Primary Intensities: Lesbian Poetry and the Reading of Difference." *What Lesbians Do in Books*. Ed. Elaine Hobby and Chris White. London: Women's Press, 1991. 28-49.

Contributors

Liahna Babener is Head of the English Department at Montana State University. Her scholarly interests include popular culture (especially film and detective fiction), regionalism, autobiography, and feminist theory, and she has published articles in all of these areas. Most recently, she edited a special number of *The Journal of Popular Culture* focusing on the film *Fatal Attraction* to which she contributed an essay. Her current projects include two edited collections of essays: one on various critical readings of the film *The Crying Game*, and the other, tentatively titled *Re-patriating the Text: Filming Feminist Stories,* addressing the ways Hollywood productions de-feminize women's novels, converting them into affirmations of the patriarchal system. She is also at work upon *Bitter Nostalgia: Recollections of Growing Up Midwestern,* a study of regional autobiographies, and is advisory editor of the literature section of the forthcoming *Encyclopedia of U.S. Popular Culture.*

Mary Jean DeMarr is Professor Emerita of English at Indiana State University, where she taught courses in American literature, popular literature, women's studies, and composition. She also served as Director of Graduate Studies. With Jane S. Bakerman, she is co-author of *Adolescent Female Portraits in the American Novel: 1961-1981: An Annotated Bibliography* and *The Adolescent in the American Novel since 1960.* She edited and contributed to *In the Beginning: First Novels in Mystery Series.* A former American Editor of the Modern Humanities Research Association's *Annual Bibliography of English Language and Literature,* she publishes regularly in the fields of detective fiction and midwestern literature, her essays most often appearing in *Clues* and *MidAmerica.*

Mary P. Freier received her Ph.D. from the University of Illinois at Urbana-Champaign in 1984. Since then, she has taught at Indiana University East, and is currently Professor of English at Dakota State University in Madison, South Dakota. She teaches American literature, composition, and interdisciplinary honors courses, as well as courses in two- and three-dimensional computer graphics. She has conducted research on nineteenth-century American literature, in particular on the

163

popular writings of nineteenth-century women, especially Mary Jane Holmes. She has also presented and published research on detective fiction. Like Hilda Adams, she does double duty—by doing free-lance graphics presentations.

Margaret Kinsman grew up in the Chicago area, studied English literature at Antioch College, and in 1970 moved to London, U.K., as Administrative Director of the Antioch London Studies Centre. Since then, she has worked as an adult literacy teacher and program director. In 1990, she joined the faculty of the Education Studies Department at South Bank University in London as a Senior Lecturer in English literature. Her particular teaching interests are women writers of the early 20th century and women crime fiction writers. Her current research interest in Sara Paretsky resulted in a paper on Paretsky at the 1994 Popular Culture Association conference in Chicago; and various speaking engagements in London. She has contributed an essay on friendship to the forthcoming *Oxford Companion to Crime and Mystery Writing*. A longer work on Paretsky and women writers of the Chicago Renaissance is in progress.

Kathleen Gregory Klein is the author of the award-winning book *The Woman Detective: Gender and Genre* (1988; rev. ed., 1995; Tokyo: 1994); and the editor of Edgar and Agatha nominee *Great Women Mystery Writers: Classic to Contemporary* (1994). She has published numerous articles on detective fiction and on feminism; she has also served on the editorial boards of *Twentieth Century Crime and Mystery Writers, The Oxford Companion to Crime and Mystery Writing*, and *Clues: A Journal of Detection*. She teaches English and Women's Studies at Southern Connecticut State University in New Haven.

Joan G. Kotker teaches English and crime fiction at Bellevue Community College in Bellevue, Washington. She is a member of the Popular Culture Association's Mystery and Detection area and has had articles and reviews published in *The Armchair Detective*. Her essays on crime fiction appear in such works as the Edgar and Agatha nominee *Great Women Mystery Writers: Classic to Contemporary; It's a Print!; In the Beginning: First Novels in Mystery Series;* and *The Oxford Companion to Crime and Mystery Writing*. She is an avid subscriber to e-mail mystery lists.

Lois A. Marchino is an Associate Professor of English at the University of Texas at El Paso. She received her B.A. and M.A. degrees from

Purdue University and her Ph.D. in literature from the University of New Mexico. Her dissertation was on the works of Doris Lessing, and she has continued to write about Lessing as well as other women writers. Among her continuing interests is detective fiction by and about women. She regularly reviews mystery novels and has presented papers at several conferences and published various articles on this topic, including "The Female Sleuth in Academe" in *The Journal of Popular Culture* and essays on Amanda Cross, Susan Conant, and Claire McNab. Dr. Marchino has served as Director of Women's Studies and is currently Director of Literature in the English department at the University of Texas at El Paso.

Sharon A. Russell is a Professor of Communication and Women's Studies and teaches film, Women's Studies, and popular culture at Indiana State University. She is a former head of the Detective and Mystery Fiction area of the Popular Culture Association. She has published many articles on popular fiction and is contributor to and editor of *The Dog Didn't Do It: Animals in Mystery* which will be published by Popular Press. She has contributed to *Great Women Mystery Writers: Classic to Contemporary*; *It's a Print*; and *In the Beginning: First Novels in Mystery Series*, and is working on a book on Stephen King.

Elizabeth A. Trembley specializes in psychological theory, modern British literature, and gothic and detective fiction. Since obtaining her Ph.D. from the University of Chicago, she has published and presented papers on Dorothy L. Sayers, Arthur Conan Doyle, medievalism, psychological theory, James Joyce, and exile and interindividuality in several British fictions. She has co-edited a book on film adaptations of detective fiction and is currently writing a study of Michael Crichton. She serves as Head of General Education at Davenport College, in Holland, Michigan, where she lives with her two German Shepherds, Morgan le Faye and Baker Street Irregular. She is also a Certified Master Trainer for dog obedience, an avocation which she finds continually enlightening in the context of her primary occupation, teaching college composition.

Priscilla L. Walton is an Associate Professor of English at Carleton University in Canada. She is the author of *Patriarchal Desire and Victorian Discourse: A Lacanian Reading of Anthony Trollope's Palliser Novels* (University of Toronto Press, 1995), and *The Disruption of the Feminine in Henry James* (University of Toronto Press, 1992). She has also published articles in such journals as the *Henry James Review, Literature/Interpretation/Theory, Commonwealth, World Literature Written in English, Victorian Review,* and *Ariel.* She is presently working on a book entitled *Detective Agency: Women Re-Writing the Hardboiled Tradition,* along with co-author Manina Jones.

Paula M. Woods, Assistant Professor of English at Baylor University in Waco, Texas, holds an M.A. from the University of Illinois and the Ph.D. from the University of North Texas. Her research and teaching interests include early women writers, sixteenth- and seventeenth-century British literature, Milton, and mystery/detective fiction. In addition to Margery Allingham and D.R. Meredith, her work in detective fiction focuses on writers of Texas and the Southwest, especially David Lindsey and Virginia Stem Owens. Her recent work includes an article on prostitution in the sixteenth-century fiction of Robert Greene (*Explorations in Renaissance Culture*) and essays on Margery Allingham in *Great Women Mystery Writers: Classic to Contemporary* and *In the Beginning: First Novels in Mystery Series.* Woods is currently completing a study of mystery novels set in the Southwest. She is a contributor to *The Oxford Companion to Crime and Mystery Writing.*